The Ultimate Guide

To The

The Legend Of Zelda:

A Link To The Past

By BlackNES Guy

Copyright © 2017 BlackNES Guy Books
All Rights Reserved

STOP!!   BEFORE GOING ANY FURTHER…

Do you like the SNES Classic??

Download our FREE *Ultimate Guide To The SNES Classic* Tips and Tricks for all 21 games!!

Go here to get a FREE digital copy

https://products.theblacknesguy.com/freebook

A Letter from BlackNES Guy

First I want to thank you for purchasing my book. Whether this is your first purchase or another one to add to your collection, I appreciate your choice. Let me introduce myself, I am the one and only BlackNES Guy, I am your average lover of video games, especially the retro games that I grew up with as a kid. When I play those games now, I think back to a simpler time when it was just me and my brother playing Super Mario World for the first time, or trying to figure out how to conquer The Legend of Zelda (without the help of the internet)! Playing those games now allows me to go back in time so to speak and relive some of those precious memories. Now being older and starting a family, I want to give my daughter the same type of experience, that is why I have created these books. They are for her as much as they are for you and me. They are designed to be a nostalgic collectable for the hardcore gamer or a simple 'old school' strategy guide to help you conquer that one game that has been eluding you all these years. Whatever your reason for buying theses books it is my goal that they help and serve you on your quest in whichever game it might be.

I have put together some additional bonuses for you inside this book. One is I invite you to join my [Facebook page](). Here we can connect and talk about retro games to our hearts content. I also love hearing any feedback you have on how to make the books even better or what guide you would like to see next! I have also included a **FREE digital download** of one of my books as a thank you for purchasing this one. You can get that by following the instructions on the next few pages. Lastly I want to tell you about my **Player 2 Press Start** team. The Player 2 Press Start team is my advance reading team. They get advance copies of my books before they are released to the public. They help make sure the book is in tip top shape by providing any additional thoughts or improvements before it goes live to the world. The most important part of being a Player 2, is when the book comes out, they leave a review on the Amazon page. Reviews are the lifeblood of my books, they let others know what you think of them. So its their job to leave reviews as soon as possible so others know how great the books are. If you want to join this team there is a link at the end of the book for you to sign up.

This is my way of giving back and adding some value to the gaming community. Video games have always been such an important part of my life and most likely yours too so I hope you enjoy my books and share them with all your gaming friends as well.

I would love to connect with you on social media as well, that info will be below :)

Thank you so much for choosing to invest your time in them.

Much love and Game On!

BlackNES Guy

www.theblacknesguy.com

Follow me on:
Twitter @blacknesguy
Facebook @ www.facebook.com/theBlackNESguy

This book is not authorized nor endorsed by Nintendo or Nintendo of America in anyway. The Nintendo logo is a trademark of Nintendo Co., Ltd. All screenshots and game art are copyright to their respective publishers. All copyright and trademarked material is reproduced under "fair use" exceptions in a transformative work.

All rights reserved. No portion of this work may be reproduced or used in any form or by any means: graphic, electronic, or mechanical, including photocopying or information storage and retrieval systems, without express written permission from the author and publisher.

The scanning, uploading and distribution of any portions of this book without the author's permission is illegal and punishable by law. Please purchase only authorized copies and do not participate in or encourage the electronic piracy of copyrighted material.

All rights reserved. No portion of this work may be reproduced or used in any form or by any means: graphic, electronic, or mechanical, including photocopying or information storage and retrieval systems, without express written permission from the author and publisher.

The scanning, uploading and distribution of any portions of this book without the author's permission is illegal and punishable by law. Please purchase only authorized copies and do not participate in or encourage the electronic piracy of copyrighted material.

For more great books check out my author page

http://www.theblacknesguy.com

More books by BlackNES Guy:

The Ultimate Guide to the NES Classic

The Ultimate Guide to Super Mario Bros

The Ultimate Guide to The Legend Of Zelda

The Ultimate Guide to The Legend Of Zelda 2

The Ultimate Guide To Castlevania

The Ultimate Guide To Castlevania 2

The Ultimate Guide to the SNES Classic

Introduction

Rescuing Princess Zelda from Hyrule Castle's dungeon will only be the beginning of Link's journey to save Hyrule in this prequel to the first two games of the Legend of Zelda franchise. Agahnim, an evil wizard, is determined to break a seal created hundreds of years ago by the Seven Sages to trap Ganon in the Dark World. Only the Master Sword can defeat Agahnim and only the chosen hero can wield the Master Sword. Link must prove he is worthy of becoming a hero if wishes to save Hyrule.

Table Of Contents

Introduction 7

History 14

Basic Gameplay 15

Enemy List 16

Prologue 34

Hyrule Castle 37

    Travel to Hyrule Castle 37

    Entering Hyrule Castle 38

    The Basement 38

    Inside Hyrule Castle 39

    BOSS BATTLE Gray Ball and Chain Trooper 41

    The Throne Room 42

    The Secret Passage 43

    The Sewers 44

    The Sanctuary 45

Eastern Palace 46

    The Lost Woods 47

    Kakariko Village - Main 49

    Kakariko Village - South 53

    Magic Powder 54

    Finding Sahasrahla (Optional) *55*

    Eastern Palace Compound *56*

    Entering Eastern Palace *58*

    Eastern Palace Dungeon Map (Optional) *58*

    Eastern Palace Dungeon Compass *60*

    The Bow *61*

    Finding Eastern Palace Boss Room *63*

    BOSS BATTLE Six Armos Knights *64*

Desert Palace **66**

    The Pegasus Boots *66*

    The Book of Mudora *67*

    The Great Swamp *68*

    The Ice Rod *71*

    The Desert of Mystery *71*

    Entering Desert Palace *72*

    Desert Palace Dungeon Map (Optional) *73*

    The Power Glove *74*

    Finding Desert Palace Boss Room *75*

    BOSS BATTLE Three Lanmolas *77*

Tower of Hera **78**

    Zora's Flippers *78*

    The Mysterious Pond (Optional) *82*

    The Pond of Happiness (Optional) *83*

Hyrulian Cemetery (Optional)	85
Finding Death Mountain	86
The Magic Mirror	86
Death Mountain	87
Entering Tower of Hera	88
The Moon Pearl	90
Finding Tower of Hera Boss Room	91
BOSS BATTLE Moldorm	93

Hyrule Castle Tower 94

The Master Sword	94
Ether Medallion	96
Return to the Sanctuary	96
Entering Hyrule Castle Tower	97
Hyrule Castle Tower	97
BOSS BATTLE Agahnim	99

Palace of Darkness 101

Quake Medallion	101
Entering the Palace of Darkness	102
The Palace of Darkness	105
Palace of Darkness Dungeon Map (Optional)	106
The Palace of Darkness Compass	108
The Magic Hammer	110
Finding the Palace of Darkness Boss Room	111

Boss Room The Helmasaur King 113

Swamp Palace 115

  Extra Items (Optional) 115

  The Flute 118

  Extra Items 2 (Optional) 120

  Bomba Medallion (Optional) 125

  Cane of Byrna (Optional) 126

  Entering Swamp Palace 127

  Swamp Palace Dungeon Map 127

  Swamp Palace Compass (Optional) 129

  The Hookshot 129

  Finding Swamp Palace Boss Room 131

  BOSS BATTLE Arrghus 134

Skull Woods 136

  Death Mountain Piece of Heart (Optional) 136

  Entering Skull Woods 137

  Skull Woods Dungeon Map and Compass (Optional) 138

  The Fire Rod 139

  Finding Skull Woods Boss Room 141

  BOSS BATTLE Mothula 143

Gargoyle's Domain 145

  Finding Gargoyle's Domain 145

  Gargoyle's Domain Dungeon Map and Compass (Optional) 146

    Gargoyle's Domain Big Key 147

    The Titan's Mitt 147

    Helping the Woman 149

    BOSS BATTLE Blind 150

Ice Palace 152

    The Tempered Sword (Optional) 152

    Extra Items 3 (Optional) 153

    Entering Ice Palace 156

    Ice Palace Dungeon Compass 156

    Ice Palace Dungeon Map 157

    The Blue Mail 161

    Opening Ice Palace Boss Room 163

    Finding Ice Palace Boss Room 165

    BOSS BATTLE Kholdstare 166

Misery Mire 168

    Entering Misery Mire 168

    Misery Mire Dungeon Compass 169

    Cane of Somaria 170

    Misery Mire Dungeon Map 173

    Finding Misery Mire Boss Room 174

    BOSS BATTLE Vitreous 176

Turtle Rock 178

    The Super Bomb 178

The Golden Sword and Silver Arrows 179

Climbing to Turtle Rock 180

Extra Items 4 (Optional) 181

Entering Turtle Rock 183

Turtle Rock Dungeon Compass (Optional) 184

Turtle Rock Dungeon Map 185

The Mirror Shield 186

Finding Turtle Rock Boss Room 188

BOSS BATTLE Trinexx 191

Ganon's Tower 193

Finding Ganon's Tower 193

Entering Ganon's Tower 194

Ganon's Tower Dungeon Map (Optional) 195

Finding the Six Armos Knights 195

MINI BOSS BATTLE Six Armos Knights 197

The Red Mail 197

Finding the Three Lanmolas 197

MINI BOSS BATTLE Three Lanmolas 199

Finding Moldorm 199

MINI BOSS BATTLE Moldorm 201

Finding Agahnim 201

BOSS BATTLE Agahnim 201

BOSS BATTLE Ganon 202

HISTORY

Since its release in 1991, *The Legend of Zelda: A Link to the Past* has sold over 4 million copies worldwide. Originally released for the Super Nintendo Entertainment System, the game has since been released for the GameBoy Advance and is digitally available on the Wii, Wii U, and Nintendo 3DS. Both the original SNES version and the slightly altered GameBoy Advance version have earned high praise.

In 1990, Nintendo Power held a contest to select a fan to appear in an upcoming game. Chris Houlihan won and what has now been termed the "Chris Houlihan Room" appeared in *A Link to the Past*. The room contains 45 Blue Rupees and a telepathy tile on the northern wall. Chris telepathically speaks to Link by saying, "I'm Chris Houlihan. This is my top secret room. Keep it between us, OK?" Although the room is considered an easter egg, it also serves a purpose as crash prevention. Link will appear in the room when the game cannot detect which room he should be in due to an error in his Y coordinate.

The third game in the Legend of Zelda franchise, *A Link to the Past* innovated the traditional storyline of the Legend of Zelda by introducing alternate worlds, the Light World and the Dark World. Parallel universes would continue to be a recurring theme in later installations in the Zelda series.

Now famous, the Master Sword makes its first appearance along with several other new weapons. Heart Containers are split into four pieces, the first time in the series. Other improvements to the game include diagonal movements, running, and sword animations. No longer does Link stab with his sword, but he can now swing. These changes make Link much easier to control and decreases the difficulty of combat.

Four Swords was later released with the GameBoy Advance remake of *A Link to the Past*. It features multiplayer gameplay where 2-4 players must solve dungeons as a team. Players compete to win the most Rupees and a special prize, though all Rupees are split evenly at the end of the dungeon.

Basic Gameplay

A *Link to the Past* uses an angled, top-down perspective on all of its screens, abandoning the side scrolling action sequences seen in *Zelda II: The Adventure of Link*. Even the overworld perspective remains the same as in dungeons, towns, and buildings. The larger overworld map can, instead, be viewed as a subscreen.

The experience system to level Link has been removed since *Zelda II*, but Heart Containers and the Magic Meter have remained. Instead of Spells, the Magic Meter is used in conjunction with items, such as the Lamp. Link can now gain Heart Containers by collecting four Pieces of Heart.

Items like Bombs and Arrows are no longer infinite. Instead, each individual item must be collected.

Link's combat techniques have improved; he now swings his sword instead of stabbing. However, lightning bolts no longer shoot from the sword. Link can also now charge his sword to produce a Spin Attack.

Travel has also been improved. Link can now walk diagonally. Once the Pegasus Boots have been obtained, Link can even run. The Magic Mirror allows Link to travel between the Dark World and the Light World through a temporary portal. Permanent, but hidden warp locations can be found in both worlds. These methods of travel allow players to solve puzzles by warping between the Light and Dark Worlds.

Enemy List

	Anti-Fairy	These enemies bounce around the room, causing damage and stealing Magic whenever they touch Link. Use the Magic Power to transform them into a Fairy.
	Archer	Types: Green, Blue Archers shoot arrows at Link whenever he draws near. Using a sword or the Bow is the most effective means of defeating them. Green Archers hide in bushes or grass and are immobile. Blue Archers move around the overworld. Blue Arches will often drop Arrows when they are defeated.
	Armos	Armos begin as stationary statues. Once Link approaches them, them come to life and hop towards Link. The most effective weapon against them is a sword.
	Babasu	Babasus are found inside of dungeons, often emerging from darkened holes in the walls. They are first seen in the Ice Palace. While they can be defeated with a single strike from the Master Sword, they are usually best to avoid. They are often found in rooms with moving floors and traps.
	Ball	Types: Regular, Giant Balls are impossible to defeat or block. They appear in palaces, continuously shooting out of walls or Wall Turrets, and Link must walk carefully to pass them. Giant Balls occasionally shoot out of holes along with the regular balls. Be cautious, as they take up more room and are more difficult to dodge.

	Ball and Chain Trooper	Types: Gray, Gold
		A Gray Ball and Chain Trooper is the first mini boss of the game, guarding Princess Zelda in Hyrule Castle. While many weapons work against them, the easiest method is to throw pots. If no pots are available, continuously hit it before it swings its weapon, then run backwards. Repeat this process until the Ball and Chain Trooper has been defeated.
	Bari	Types: Blue, Red, Biri
		Vulnerable to the Bow, Hookshot, and any sword, Baris are floating creatures that occasionally emit electric shocks. Avoid attacking them when they are electrified.
		Blue Baris are the weaker of the two.
		Red Baris are stronger and move faster than Blue Baris. Once they have been attacked, they will split into two Biris. These Biris are just as strong as the Red Baris, but much smaller.
	Beamos	[Trap] The Beamos is a stationary enemies that constantly rotates its laser beam-shooting eye. It is indestructible. The best method for dealing with a Beamos is to avoid it or use the Mirror Shield to reflect the laser beams.
	Bee	Types: Regular, Good/Golden
		Bees are often found when Link hits a tree with a dash attack. They appear in groups as well as by themselves. Link can catch them with the Bug-Catching Net and hold them in jars. When a bee is released from a jar, it will attack nearby enemies before flying off.
		The Good/Golden Bee is blue. When released, it will not fly away from enemies. It can also be sold in Kakariko Village for one hundred rupees.

	Blade Trap	Types: Regular, Giant
		[Trap] First appearing in the Palace of Darkness, Blade Traps are undefeatable. Often, they move horizontally across rooms. Giant Blade Traps are triggered by motion, but move more slowly than the regular ones.
	Bomb Knight	Bomb Knights guard Hyrule Castle after Princess Zelda has been rescued. They throw bombs at Link whenever he gets too close. They are more annoying than dangerous, so they can be avoided. However, they are vulnerable to swords and Bombs.
	Boulder	[Trap] Found rolling down Death Mountain, Boulders do damage whenever they touch Link. They are invincible and should be avoided.
	Bumper	[Trap] First appearing in the Tower of Hera, Bumpers are stationary traps. Although they do no damage, touching one will push Link in the opposite direction. This can cause problems with other enemies, traps, or holes in the floor. Avoid touching them as much as possible.
	Buzz	Buzz are the Dark World versions of Rats. They often appear in groups. Slash them with a sword to defeat them.
	Buzz Blob	Link will take damage from a Buzz Blob if he tries to immediately attack. To defeat them, first stun them with the Boomerang or Hookshot, then attack them with a sword. Use the Magic Powder on a Buzz Blob to turn it into a Cukeman.

	Chain Chomp	[Trap] While the chain does not hurt Link, the ball of the Chain Chomp can do a lot of damage. Since these traps are invincible, avoid the Chain Chomps. The Cane of Byrna or the Magic Cape can be used.
	Chasupa	Identical to Kesse enemies, Chasupas perch on walls and fly towards Link when he gets too close. Use the Boomerang or a sword to defeat them.
	Crow	Cros swoop down from trees and attack Link when he passes. Use a sword to defeat them.
	Cucco	Types: Regular, Bone If Link attacks a Cucco too many times, a large group of Cuccos will attack Link. Otherwise, they are harmless. Cuccos are invincible, so don't attack them.
	Cukeman	Cukemans appear when Magic Powder is used on Buzz Blobs. Although they can still hurt Link, they can be defeated with a sword, Hookshot, Boomerang, or Bow. Unlike all other enemies, Link can interact with Cukemans. They will say random phrases. If the Ice Rod or Ether Medallion is used to freeze them, then the Magic Hammer is used to smash them, they will transform back into Buzz Blobs.
	Dacto	Dactos are more aggressive than their Light World counterparts, Crows. They perch on top of trees and attack when Link walks to close. It is best to avoid them or defeat them with a strike from a sword.
	Deadrock	Deadrocks cannot be defeated, but only stunned. If Link uses Magic

		Powder or the Quake Medallion on them, they will turn into Slime.
	Devalant	Types: Blue, Red Devalants are stationary, burrowing and emerging from the same location. They can pull Link into their holes. The only way for Link to escape is to defeat them. Devalants can be damaged by the Ice Rod, Bow, or swords. Red Devalants have the ability to shoot unblockable fireballs.
	Eyegore	Types: Green, Red Eyegores begin as stationary statues. Once approached, they open their eyes and move towards Link. The most effective method to defeat an Eyegore is to use a pot or an Arrow. A sword will also do damage, but it will require several hits. Red Eyegores have higher health than Green ones, but they deal the same amount of damage.
	Fireball Cannon	[Trap] These stationary traps remain harmless unless Link swings a sword. When this happens, the Fireball Cannon will shoot fireballs in four directions. Although they are not very threatening on their own, they are often found with other enemies and traps. Link cannot defeat them, so they are best to avoid.
	Flying Tile	[Trap] Flying Tiles rise from the floor and fly toward Link. They can be avoided by dodging or defeated by slash with a sword. They are found in large groups (18-20) and take turn attacking Link. Once they have struck an item or wall, they will be defeated.
	Freezor	Freezors begin as statues on the walls of the Ice Palace. When Link walk in front of one, it will free itself and charge. Not all Freezor statues will become Freezor enemies. Only the Fire Rod or the Bombos

		Medallion can defeat them.
	Geldman	Only appear outside of Desert Palace, Geldman emerge from the ground and move quickly towards Link. After burrowing back underground, they will reappear in their original location. Although the Boomerang and a sword can damage Geldman, they are best to be avoided as they are usually accompanied by other enemies
	Gibdo	Found in the Skull Woods dungeon, Gibdos move slowly in straight lines. They are often found in groups and require many hits to be defeated. Since they are mummies, they are vulnerable to fire. The easiest way to defeat them is with the Fire Rod or the Bombos Medallion.
	Gibo	Types: Regular, Water Gibos are made of two parts, the body and its cloud. The body will detach itself from the cloud and try to attack Link. Afterwards, it will rejoin the cloud. Link must attack the body when it is detached. Use a sword or the Bow to defeat this enemy. Water Gibos are much more difficult to defeat. They must first be frozen with the Ice Rod or Ether Medallion and then whacked with the Magic Hammer. If Link tries to defeat it without freezing it, the Water Gibo will respawn.
	Goriya	Types: Green, Red Goriyas are found in many Legend of Zelda games, but are drastically different in *A Link to the Past*. In this game, they mirror Links movements. Green Goriyas have no attack, though they will do damage if Link touches them. Most weapons will defeat them. Red Goriyas do not perfect mirror Link's movements. North and south movements are mirrored, while right and left exactly follow

		Link's movements. They also have the ability to shoot fireballs when directly facing Link. Red Goriyas are also invulnerable to everything except arrows.
	Guruguru Bar	[Trap] Guruguru Bars are Winders that are permanently set to revolve around an object. They are indestructible and should be avoided.
	Hardhat Beetle	Types: Blue, Red The most dangerous aspect of Hardhat Beetles is that Link will slide backwards after attacking one. They can be stunned with the Hookshot or Bombs. When they are stunned, Link can attack without worrying about sliding backwards. Red Hardhat Beetles have more health than Red ones.
	Helmasaur	Helmasaurs charge directly at Link. Their green mask prevents damage, so Link must use a sword on their vulnerable body. The Magic Hammer can defeat them in one hit, regardless of where the Helmasaur is hit. Magic Powder can be used to transform them into Slime.
	Hinox	Although Hinox toss bombs randomly and move slowly, if Link gets too close they will charge and aim their bombs at Link. Touching the Hinox will do more damage than the Hinox's bombs. These enemies can be defeated with a single Bomb. Alternatively, it will take several hits with a sword or Arrow to defeat them.
	Hoarder	Hoarders are shy creatures that hide beneath bushes or boulders. Once discovered, they will move away from Link, dropping rupees in the process. Link can defeat them with a single slash from any sword.

	Name	Description
	Hokkubokku	The easiest way to defeat a Hokkubokku is with a single hit from the Fire Rod or the Bombos Medallion. If Link uses a sword, the Hokkubokku will break apart into segments. Each of these pieces will bounce around the room. Link must defeat each piece individually. If a piece hits a wall three times, it will also be defeated.
	Hover	Appearing only in the Swamp Palace, hovers have the ability to glide on water. They move in short bursts before resting and can only move diagonally. While they usually appear in groups, Link can easily defeat them with the Master Sword. They cannot travel on land, only on water.
	Hyu	The Dark World versions of Poes, Hyus haunt the Village of Outcasts and Skeleton Forest. Though they don't actively attack Link, they can do damage if contact is made. Defeat them with almost all of Link's weapons.
	Kesse	Kesse perch on wall until Link walks too close, then they swoop down. They are easy to defeat with one hit from most weapons.
	Kodongo	Types: Red, Green Red Kodongos are found in the Tower of Hera, while Green Kodongos are found in the Palace of Darkness. They both have the ability to shoot burst of three fireballs from their mouths. These fireballs will continue to burn even after they have stopped moving. While there is very little difference between Red and Green Kodongos, Green Kodongos prefer the darkness. Both can be defeated with a single hit from a sword.
	Ku	Kus are the Dark World variants of River Zora. They emerge from the water to shoot fireballs, then dive back down. Ku will resurface in

		another part of the water. The Fire Shield can deflect their fireballs and the enemies can be defeated with most of the weapons.
	Laser Eye	[Trap] Laser eyes first appear in Misery Mire. They are stationary traps, located on dungeon walls. When Link walks in front of them, they will shoot lasers. They cannot be defeated, but the Mirror Shield can block their lasers.
	Leever	Types: Green, Purple Leevers emerge from the ground and spin towards Link. Eventually, they will burrow back underground only to pop up somewhere else. They can be defeated with any sword. Purple Leevers are quicker than Green Leevers, but deal and receive the same amount of damage.
	Lynel	Only found near Ganon's Tower, Lynels shoot fireballs. The Fire Shield cannot deflect these, but the Mirror Shield can. Lynels cannot be damaged from a regular attack with the Master Sword. Link must use a spin attack or stronger swords. The Magic Hammer and Silver Arrows can also damage this enemy.
	Medusa	[Trap] Medusas are stationary traps that shoot fireballs. These fireballs can be deflected with the Fire Shield. Medusas cannot be defeated, so avoid them.
	Mini-Moldorm	These enemies move quickly and erratically. Use a sword to defeat them. Alternatively, use the dash attack to avoid them.
	Moblin	Moblins are the Dark World equivalent to the Light World's various types of soldiers. They toss Trident spears at Link whenever he gets too close. The Fire Shield can deflect these Trident and one hit from the Master Sword will defeat the Moblin. Use the Magic Powder to

		turn them into Slime.
	Octoballon	The Octoballon is only found on the southeast side of Lake Hylia. It is a bloated Octorok that floats above the earth. Eventually it will burst, causing eight mini Octoroks to appear. This mini Octoroks will quickly disappear, so it is best to momentarily avoid them. They can easily be defeated with any sword.
	Octorok	Octoroks have two different types base on two different attacks, though both types look identical. The first type will shoot a single projectile when Link crosses its path. The second type will shoot multiple projectiles in a circle. Both types can be defeated with a single hit from any sword.
	Pengator	Found in groups, Pengators run and dive onto the ice to slide into Link. They can be defeated with the Fire Rod or Bombos Medallion. Due to their appearance in groups, the Bombos Medallion is the prefered method to defeat them.
	Pikit	Pikits can be found in the Dark World around Ice Lake, Skeleton Forest, and the Plains of Ruin. They hop towards Link and can steal items with such as rupees, Bombs, Arrows, the Fighter's Shield, and the Fire Shield with their long tongue. Link will need to defeat the Pikit before it steals a second item. If the Pikit does steal another item, the first item will be unrecoverable. Defeat them with any sword.
	Pikku	Like the Thieves of the Light World, Pikkus cannot be defeated. They ram into Link, causing him to drop rupees, Bombs, and Arrows. Avoid them if possible or be quick to collect the fallen items if the Pikku cannot be avoided.

	Pirogusu	Only found in the Swamp Palace, emerge from holes in the palace walls. Although they can be defeated with the Master Sword, they will keep spawning from the walls. They are best to avoid when possible.
	Poe	Found only in the Hyrulian Graveyard, Poes are best to avoid. They do not actively attack Link, but cause damage if contact is many. It will take many hits to defeat them, though they can take damage from most of Link's weapons.
	Popo	Popo are one of the rare enemies that can appear in both the Light and Dark Worlds. However, they are not very dangerous and can be defeated with one hit from almost any weapon. The move slowly and inch closer to Link.
	Rabbit Beam	[Trap] Often found hiding under items or skulls, Rabbit Beams are traps that have the ability to transform Link into a rabbit for a few seconds. When Link is a Rabbit, he cannot use any weapons. They are usually easy to avoid, but can be defeated with any of the medallions.
	Rat	Rats usually travel in groups and can be defeated with one hit from the Fighter's Sword.
	River Zora	River Zora pop up from the water in much of the Light World overworld. Most River Zorashoot fireballs that can be deflected with the Fire or Mirror Shield. Some of the River Zora in Zora's Lake can walk towards Link while in the shallow water. Most of the time, it is best to avoid the River Zoras. However, they can be defeated with any sword, the Ice Rod, or the Bombos Medallion.
	Ropa	Ropas move slowly and jump towards Link. They are only found in the Dark World and can easily defeated with any sword.

	Rope	Only found in dungeons, Ropes rush towards Link. They move quickly, but can be defeated with any sword.
	Sand Crab	Sand Crabs can be found along bodies of water in the Light World. They move fast when traveling sideways, but slow when traveling vertically. A single hit from any sword will defeat them.
	Slarok	The Dark World versions of Octoroks, Slaroks attack in an identical fashion. Only one hit from the Master Sword will defeat them. They are found near the shores of Ice Lake.
	Slime	When Link uses the Quake Medallion or the Magic Powder on certain enemies, they will turn into Slimes. These enemies are quite weak and can be defeated by a single sword slash.
	Sluggula	Sluggulas leave a trail of bombs behind them when they move. They are not vulnerable to their own bombs or Link's Bombs. Use the Master Sword to defeat them.
	Snap Dragon	Often found around other types of enemies, Snap Dragons hop around Link. If Link gets too close, they will charge towards him. They can only move diagonally, however, and the Magic Powder can be used on them to transform them into Slime. It will take three hits with the Master Sword to defeat them.
	Soldier	Although Soldiers also come in a variety of colors and specialties, regular Soldiers are the weakest. They move back and forth, making no attempt to attack Link. Avoid them or hit the with any sword to defeat them.
	Spark	[Trap] Sparks fly from torches in many of the dungeons, beginning with the Tower of Hera. They are invincible and should be avoided.

	Spear Knight	Spear Knights are protected by more armor than their Spear Soldier counterparts. They also wield a Trident. Unlike Spear Soldiers, Spear Knights do not charge at Link. They throw an infinite of Tridents from a distance. Although they can easily be avoided, hitting them with any sword will defeat them.
	Spear Soldier	Types:Green, Red Spear Soldiers do twice as much damage as Sword Soldiers. They charge towards Link in an attempt to hit him with their spear. Once Link defeats Agahnim for the first time, Red Sword Soldiers will appear all over the Light World. Red Spear Soldiers have a higher amount of health than Green Spear Soldiers. Use any sword to defeat them.
	Spear Throwing Soldier	Like Archers, Spear Throwing Soldiers hide in the grass and only pop up to throw their spears at Link. They are often found near Bomb Knights. The Bomb Knight's bomb can defeat the Spear Throwing Soldier if it lands close enough. Link can also defeat them with any sword, but they are easy to avoid.
	Spiked Roller	[Trap] Spiked Rollers are only found in Turtle Rock. They move back and forth across a room. Because they are invincible, Link should avoid them.
	Stal	Stals hide in the Dark World, appearing as harmless skulls or hiding under bushes. When Link gets too close, they come alive and hop towards him. One hit from the Master Sword will defeat them. The Magic Powder can also be used on them to turn them into Slimes.
	Stalfos	Types: Blue, Gray, Red, Yellow, Green, Orange Stalfos come in a variety of colors and types, each with their own style

		of attack. Blue Stalfos are the simplest. They move around a room, not actively attacking Link. However, they will jump back when Link tries to attack them, so they must be cornered. Magic Powder can be used on Blue Stalfos to turn them into Slimes. Gray and Yellow Stalfos toss their spinning heads at Link. Once the heads have been removed from the body, the heads cannot be defeated. Attack only the bodies while avoiding the heads. Eventually, the heads will float off screen and vanish. Red Stalfos move like Blue Stalfos, but toss a spinning bone at Link after jumping away. Green and Orange Stalfos do not have bodies. Instead, they are floating heads that move slowly towards Link.
	Stalfos Knight	Stalfos Knight drop from the ceiling and look in both directions to find their prey. While Link can defeat them with enough sword slashes or enough hits with the Boomerang, there is a much more efficient method. Hit them with a sword once and they will crumple. Next, use a Bomb to defeat them.
	Stalrope	The Dark World counterparts to Ropes, Stalropes are only found in a single room in Gargoyle's Domain. They slither towards Link and can be defeated with a single sword slash.
	Swamola	Swamolas are only found inside the Swamp of Evil in the Dark World. They jump out of the water, fly through the air, and dive back into the water. Their movements are identical to their land cousins, Lanmolas. While they can be defeated with a sword, it is best to avoid them since they do a large amount of damage.

	Sword Knight	Stronger than Sword Soldiers, Sword Knights immediately charge at Link. Defeat them using any sword.
	Sword Soldier	Types: Green, Blue While Sword Soldiers patrol areas like regular Soldiers, Sword Soldiers will charge towards Link. Despite having a shield, the shield will not block Link's attacks. Their sword, however, can block. Link can attack with a sword, pot, or stun them with the Boomerang. Green Sword Soldiers will often hide in bushes and pop out when Link walks too close. Blue Sword Soldiers have more health than Green Sword Soldiers. After Link has defeated Agahnim the first time, they will begin to appear in Kakariko Village.
	Tarosu	Types: Blue, Red Tarosus are the Dark World variant of Sword Soldiers and can be defeated in the same manner. Their attacks and actions are almost identical. Blue Tarosus act like Green Sword Soldiers and Red Tarosus act like Blue Sword Soldiers.
	Tektite	Types: Blue, Red Tektites jump Towards Link in an attempt to cause damage. They can be defeated with almost any weapon. Red Tektites are faster and have more health than Blue Tektites.
	Terrorpin	The hard shell on a Terrorpin's back protects it from damage. To defeat this enemy, use the Magic hammer on or near the Terrorpin. This will flip the enemy upside down. Link can then use the Magic Hammer or a sword to defeat it. Be careful because the Terrorpin will flip back over after a few seconds. Striking the ground with the Magic Hammer

		a second time will cause the Terrorpin to flip back over on its feet.
	Thief	Thieves charge at Link in an attempt to steal items such as rupees, Bombs, and Arrows. While Thieves cannot cause damage to Link, Link cannot defeat them. Instead, avoid them. If a Thief hits Link, quickly collect the dropped items.
	Toppo	Toppo only exist in the Great Swamp before Link has defeated Agahnim for the first time. They pop up from the grass, burrow down, and pop up from another location. This may seem random, but each Toppo only has four places it can pop out of. They can easily be defeated with a sword. However, Link can get valuable items from them if he slashes the grass that the Toppo will emerge from. The Toppo will be unable to burrow back down. Speak to it and it will give Link either rupees, a heart, a Fairy, a big Magic Jar, Bombs, or Arrows.
	Vulture	Vultures are only found within the Desert of Mystery. When Link get too close, they leave their perches to circle around him. Link will only be injured if he walks into the circling Vulture. These enemies can be defeated with most weapons.
	Wallmaster	Despite their name, Wallmasters drop from the ceiling of dungeons and attempt to grab Link. Before they drop, a shadow will appear on the ground and a noise can be heard. If they are able to grab Link, he will return to the most recent dungeon entrance. Wallmasters can be defeated with a sword, but new Wallmasters will continue to drop from the ceiling. It is best to avoid them.
	Wall Turret	[Trap] Turrets are invincible and consistently shoot Balls as they move. Avoid the projectiles.

	Winder	[Trap] Winders consist of five fire balls and travel along walls. They are easy to predict as the move in a straight direction, turning only when they touch something. They cannot be defeated or stunned, so avoid them.
	Wizzrobe	Types: Regular, Blue Both the regular and Blue Wizzrobe act identically, despite their clothing preferences. Wizzrobes appear, shoot energy beams, and fade. Each time they appear, the face towards Link. Link can defeat them with a sword, any of the medallions, or the Cane of Somaria.
	Zazak	Types: Blue, Red Zazaks wander around the room slowly and can easily be defeated with a single hit from a sword. Red Zazaks shoot powerful fireballs that can only be deflected with the Mirror Shield. They also have slightly more health than Blue Zazaks.
	Zirro	Types: Blue, Green Zirros hover around Ice Lake. When Link gets close, they hover nearby in an erratic pattern. They can be defeated with a sword, or the Bow. Blue Zirros can only damage Link by touching him. If Link attempts to hit the Blue Zirro, it will begin to fly away. Green zirros can rapidly shoot seeds. These seeds create a small explosion when they hit the ground. Although they have the ability to attack, they have lower health than Blue Zirros.
	Zol	Types: Red, Green, Yellow, Dark Green Although Zols come in many colors, they all act identically. Zols are slow moving, but will occasionally jump towards Link. They are found only in dungeons and can be defeated with most weapons.

	Zoro	When Link blows open certain holes in Misery Mire and Turtle Rock, a group of Zoros will emerge. They will move in a straight path until they hit a wall and vanish. New groups of Zoros will continuously emerge from the hole. Although they are easily defeated with a sword, it is best to avoid them because more will always spawn.

Prologue

The Legends of Hyrule

To set the stage for this adventure of the legendary Hero of Hyrule, it will be informative to delve into the Triforce myth, an ancient epic about the creation of the world that is still believed in the land of Hyrule. Every culture has such myths and theories about the creation of their worlds, and it can be beneficial and entertaining to examine them in detail, for they often affect the present day social structure. The legends say the mythical gods of Hyrule had as their chosen people the Hylia. These ancient people left scrolls that are the primary source of the legends.

The Creation of Hyrule

According to the Hyrule scrolls, the mythical gods descended from a distant nebula to the world and created order and life. The God of Power dyed the mountains red with fire and created land. The God of Wisdom created science and wizardry and brought order to nature. And the God of Courage, through justice and vigor, created life – the animals that crawl the land and the birds that soar in the sky. After the gods had finished their work, they left the world, but not before creating a symbol of their strength, a golden triangle known as the Triforce. A small but powerful portion of the essence of the gods was held in this mighty artifact, which was to guide the intelligent life on the world of Hyrule.

Although it was an inanimate object, the Triforce had the power to bestow three titles which gave the person who received them great powers: "The Forger of Strength", "The Keeper of Knowledge", and "The Juror of Courage". From its hiding place in the so-called Golden Land where the Gods placed it, the Triforce beckoned people from the outside world to seek it in the hope that someone worthy of these titles would find it. With their magic infused blood, the Hylian people were endowed with psychic powers and skill in wizardry. It was also said that their long, pointed ears enabled them to hear special messages from the gods, so they were held in high esteem by many people in Hyrule. Their descendants settled in various parts of the world and passed on their knowledge and magical lore to all people. But in its passing, the lore was often distorted or lost altogether...

Gates to the Golden Land

In Hyrule, there are many Hylianbuildings which are mentioned repeatedly in the legends. These buildings, which now lie in ruin, pale shadows of their former splendor, are closely tied to the Triforce. Some were even said to house the Triforce...

If it were only a symbol of the gods, the Triforce would be coveted by many. But a verse from the Book of Mudora (a collection of Hylian legends and lore) made the Triforce even more desirable:

In a realm beyond sight,

The sky shines gold, not blue.

There, the Triforce's might

Makes mortal dreams come true.

Many aggressively searched for the wish-granting Triforce, but no one, not even the Hylian sages, was sure of its location; the knowledge had been lost over time. Some said the Triforce lay under the desert, others said it was in the cemetery in the shadow of Death Mountain, but no one ever found it. That yearning for the Triforce soon turned to lust for power, which in turn led to the spilling of blood. Soon, the only motive left among those searching for the Triforce was pure greed.

One day, quite by accident, a gate to the Golden Land of the Triforce was opened by a gang of thieves skilled in the black arts. This land was like no other. In the gathering twilight, the Triforce shone from its resting place high above the world. In a long running battle, the leader of the thieves fought his way past his followers in a lust for the Golden Power. After vanquishing his own followers, the leader stood triumphant over the Triforce and grasped it with his blood-stained hands. He heard a whispered voice: "If thou has a strong desire or dream, wish for it..." And in reply, the roaring laughter of the brigand leader echoed across time and space and even reached the far-off land of Hyrule. The name of this king of thieves is GanondorfDragmire, but he is known by his alias, MandragGanon, which means Ganon of the Enchanted Thieves.

The Imprisoning War

I do not know what Ganon wished for from the Triforce. However, in time evil power began to flow from the Golden Land and greedy men were drawn there to become members of Ganon's army. Black clouds permanently darkened the sky, and many disasters beset Hyrule. The lord of Hyrule sent for the Seven Wise Men and the Knights Of Hyrule, and ordered them to seal the entrance to the Golden Land.

The Triforce, being an inanimate object, cannot judge between good and evil. Therefore, it could not know that Ganon's wishes were evil; it merely granted them. Suspecting that Ganon's power was based on the Triforce's magic, the people of Hyrule forged a sword resistant to magic which could repulse even powers granted by the Triforce. This mighty weapon became known as the blade of evil's bane, or the Master Sword. It was so powerful that only one who was pure of heart and strong of body and mind could wield it. As the Seven Wise Men searched for a valiant person to take up the Master Sword, Ganon's evil army swarmed from the tainted Golden Land into Hyrule and attacked the castle. The wise men and the Knights of Hyrule combined forces to wage war on this evil horde.

The Knights took the full brunt of the fierce attack, and although they fought courageously many a brave soul was lost that day. However, their lives were not lost in vain, for they bought precious time for the Seven Wise Men to magically seal Ganon in the Golden Land. All of Hyrule rejoiced at the victory that upheld peace and order over Ganon's evil and chaos. This war, which had claimed many lives, became known as the Imprisoning War in stories told in later centuries.

The Coming of the Wizard

Many centuries have passed since the Imprisoning War. The land of Hyrule healed its wounds and the people lived in peace for a long time. Memories of the vicious Imprisoning War faded over the generations...

So it is no surprise that no one was prepared for the new disasters that have recently struck Hyrule. Pestilence and drought, uncontrollable even by magic, ravaged the land. The King of Hyrule, after counsel with his sages, ordered an investigation of the Imprisoned Dark World (as the Golden Land had come to be known) but the wise men's seal was apparently intact. He offered rewards for anyone who could find the source of these troubles. In answer to these summons, a stranger named Agahnim came and quelled the disasters with a previously unseen form of magic. As a reward, the king gave him a new position as chief advisor and heir to the Seven Wise Men. The masses proclaimed him their hero. Peace had returned to Hyrule... or had it?

Of late, rumors have traveled their whispering path with alarming frequency. Rumors saying Agahnim now rules the country with his magic... Rumors of strange magical experiments in the castle tower at night... The people of Hyrule were gripped by dread.

Hyrule Castle

Total Life   3

Heart Pieces   0/24

The first stage of *A Link to the Past* focuses on rescuing Princess Zelda who is imprisoned inside of Hyrule Castle's dungeon. Link must leave his home in the middle of the night and sneak into the castle's basement. Once inside, he will face soldiers and monsters. The first boss guards Princess Zelda outside of her cell. Link must defeat him to free the princess. Together, the two of them must exit the castle through a secret passage in the Throne Room.

A Link to the Past opens with a brief history of Hyrule and it's relationship with the Golden Land. The tale foreshadows Link's destiny to once again save Hyrule from the evil Ganon.

Link awakens in the middle of the night, startled by a telepathic message sent from Princess Zelda. She tells the hero that she has been locked inside of Hyrule Castle's dungeon. Link's uncle has also risen in the middle of the night. Though the uncle is carrying a sword and shield, he orders Link to remain in the house. Like any decent hero, Link ignores his uncle.

Travel to Hyrule Castle

After the cut scenes have been completed, hop out of bed and open the treasure chest in the lower right corner to receive the Lamp.

Next, exit the house and travel north through the rainy night. The house is built on a raised portion of land, but Link can jump off of the platform without becoming injured. After encountering a fence that stops Link's progress northward, travel left to cross a bridge. At the end of the bridge is Hyrule Castle. A soldier guards the front door, blocking Link's entrance.

Entering Hyrule Castle

To sneak in, walk around the right side of the castle wall and follow the path to the north. In front of a tree is a solitary bush surrounded by paving stones. Lift up the bush to discover a tunnel underneath. Drop into the hole to enter the basement of Hyrule Castle.

The Basement

Follow the path to find Link's uncle. Although he is unhappy Link has left the house, he will give Link his Fighter's Sword and Fighter's Shield. Continue to follow the passage through an open door.

Travel left, using the newly equipped sword to defeat the two Green Sword Soldiers. At the end of the room is a treasure chest containing one Blue Rupee worth 5 Rupees. Smash the pots by throwing them to find two Green Potions. It is optional to light the torch to the left of the pots by using the Lamp. Travel left, down the pathway Link used to enter the area. Travel up the stairs to the south and exit into a courtyard. Link is now within the palace walls, but outside of the castle itself.

Slash the bushes with the sword and travel to the left. Green Sword Soldiers patrol the area. Defeat them or avoid them and enter the castle door to the north.

Inside Hyrule Castle

Hyrule castle has many doors, stairs, passageways, and rooms. The most efficient way to complete the castle is to first take the door to the left on the main floor.

In the next room, follow the red carpet to travel north through an open door. Link will discover a long, narrow hallway with three Green Sword Soldiers. Defeat them and smash the two pots at the end of the hallway.

Continue through the door to the left into another narrow hallway. Midway through the room is a stairway leading downwards. Travel down it to enter a room with a Blue Sword Soldier and a treasure chest.

Defeat the Blue Sword Soldier and he will drop a key. Open the treasure chest to obtain a dungeon map. Use the key to open the lock to door to the south and travel through it.

In the next room, take the stairs down words towards the Blue Sword Soldier. Avoid or defeat him and continue south. There are two more Blue Sword Soldiers and two pots in this room. Be careful not to get too close to the edge, as Link will fall off and lose one heart. The Blue Sword Soldiers can be avoided or defeated here. Knocking them towards the edge will cause them to fall off. The pots can also be thrown at them to knock them off of the edge of the floor. If Link uses this technique, he will not be able to collect the items inside of the pots. Continue traveling south to another pot and another Blue Sword Soldier.

Follow the path left to the next room. Two Green Sword Soldiers patrol here. Avoid or defeat them and enter the door to the north.

Once Link is inside the next room, the doors will automatically lock. Defeat the Green Sword Soldier and the door Link entered through as well as the door to the right will open. Travel through the door to the right.

Again, the door will lock behind Link. Defeat the Blue Sword Soldier to unlock the door and receive a key. Open the treasure chest to collect the Boomerang. Make sure to equip the Boomerang now. Exit the room through the now unlocked door. Unlock the door on the north side of the room using the key.

Take two sets of stairs down to the next room. Again, take another set of stairs further down.

Although the Green Sword Soldier in this room can be avoided, it is recommended to defeat him. Continue left to encounter the first boss, Ball and Chain Trooper. Princess Zelda is being held in a locked cell beside him.

BOSS BATTLE Gray Ball and Chain Trooper

Gray Ball and Chain Trooper is a slow moving enemy that swings a spiked ball attached to a chain. There are three main ways to defeat him. The first is to use the three pots in the first jail cell to throw at him. Hitting him with two of these will defeat him. The second way is to stun him with the Boomerang and then slash him with the sword until he has been defeated. The final tactic is to time Link's sword slashes with his movements. The optimal way to do this is to attack once or twice when he is moving, then back up while he swings his weapon. Repeat this process until he has been defeated.

Once Gray Ball and Chain Trooper has been defeated, he will drop a Big Key. Use this to unlock Princess Zelda's cell. Open the treasure chest for a Blue Rupee, then speak to Princess Zelda. It is Link's duty to help her exit the palace.

The Throne Room

With Princess Zelda following closely behind, exit the cell room by traveling back up the three sets of stairs. Upon entering the room with the three locking doors, continue south. This is the room with the two Green Sword Soldiers from earlier. If they were defeated earlier, the room will be empty. If not, avoid or defeat them. Travel up the stairs to the south and follow the pathway left and north. Once the path comes to a dead end, jump down.

Depending on whether or not he was defeated, a Blue Sword Soldier may patrol the area. Avoid or defeat him and travel up the stairs. Enter the door to the left.

The Blue Sword Soldier in this room will have respawned. Avoid or defeat him and continue north. In the next hallway with the two statues, travel left through the doorway. Head through the doorway to the south while avoiding or defeating three Green Sword Soldiers.

In the next room is another Green Sword Soldier who can be avoided or defeated. Follow the red carpet down and exit the room through the doorway to the left.

Take the stairs immediately to the north of the door Link enters through to avoid two green Sword Soldiers. The stairway up in the middle of the north side of the room to enter the Throne Room.

Defeat or avoid two Blue Sword Soldiers and follow the red carpet to an ornamental shelf behind the chairs. Equip the Lamp, then push the shelf from the left side to open a dark entryway.

The Secret Passage

Enter the secret passageway in almost complete darkness. Rats scurry around this room. Avoid or defeat them. Travel left to light a torch next to a pot. Torches will go out if Link moves through the rooms too slowly. The next torch to light is to the north, just above two pots. Next, travel left to light a third torch. It is also near a single pot. Take the stairs downward on the northeastern side of the room.

South and to the right is another torch to be lit. This room is filled with Ropes. It is best to defeat all or most of them since the passage is too narrow to avoid them. Follow the passage left and through the next door.

This room also contains Ropes and Keeses. These can be defeated or avoided. Travel north and to the left to find a treasure chest containing a key. Light the two torches near the treasure chest and travel north through the locked door.

The Sewers

Link and Princess Zelda have now entered the sewers of Hyrule castle. This room contains many Rats to be defeated or avoided. To the right of the door is another torch. Light it and travel to the left to exit the room.

The next room contains Rats and Keeses. In the bottom left corner is a torch. Light it. Avoid or defeat the enemies and travel through the door to the north.

This room is already lit enough for Link to see, but there are two optional torches that can be lit. Defeat the Rats and Keeses until one of them drops a key. Use the key to unlock the door to the north and travel through it.

The next room is completely lit and contains no torches. However, there are many Bats and Keeses to be avoided or defeated. Travel north to the four blocks blocking a stairway. Push the middle on north to create an opening for Link and Princess Zelda to walk through. Take the stairs up.

Four pots and several Rats fill the next room. Avoid or defeat the enemies and exit through the door to the south.

Upon entering the next room, the door will automatically close and lock. Avoid or defeat the Rats. Then, pull one of the levers on the wall to open the door. Travel south to the Sanctuary.

The Sanctuary

The Sage in the Sanctuary will tell Link of his duty to defeat the wizard and prevent the releasing of the seal of seven wise men. He tells Link of the Master Sword and that it is the only weapon powerful enough to defeat the wizard. The Sage is even kind enough to mark the sword's location on the overworld map.

Open the treasure chest in the Sanctuary to receive a Heart Container. Swap your Lamp for the Boomerang then follow the red carpet south to exit the Sanctuary.

Eastern Palace

Total Life   4

Heart Pieces   0/24

Now tasked with saving Hyrule, the next portion of the game focuses on obtaining the Master Sword. Unfortunately, Link must prove that his is worthy to wield it. In order to prove his worthiness, Link must collect three Pendants of Virtue: the Pendant of Courage, the Pendant of Power, and the Pendant of Wisdom. The first pendant, the green Pendant of Courage is located in Eastern Palace. Link must face the enemies within Eastern Palace to collect the pendant and become one step closer to wielding the Master Sword.

Bring up the overworld map subscreen to view point marked by the Sage. This is Eastern Palace, the next dungeon and the location the Master Sword. However, there are a few things to collect before entering Eastern Palace.

Travel south from the sanctuary and then east, following the dirt pathway. Enemies will be patrolling the areas. The first is a Blue Sword Soldier. He can be avoided or defeated. The next section is filled with Green Sword Soldiers. Continue to the left, avoiding or defeating them as necessary.

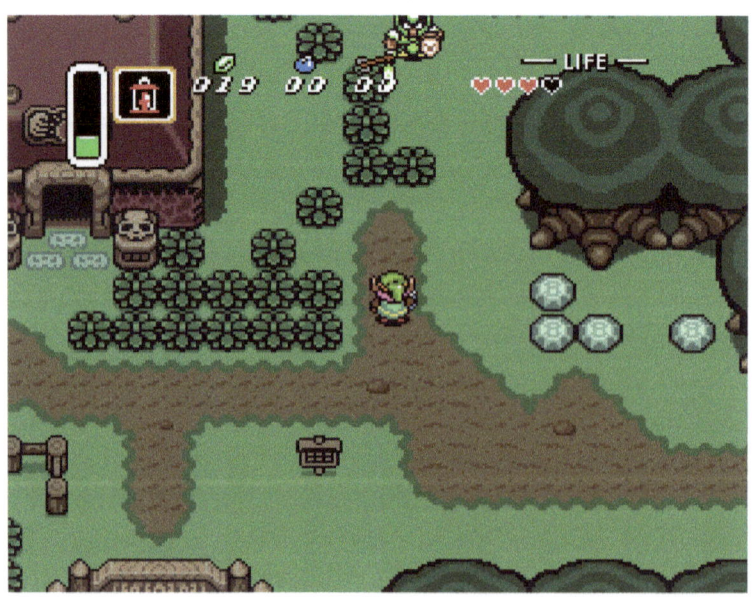

In the third section, marked by a gateway to the south, immediately travel north towards two Green Sword Soldiers. It is easiest to defeat them before continuing north and entering a gap in the trees.

The Lost Woods

An enemy Crow perches on a nearby tree. Avoid or defeat him while traveling north. Upon reaching a small, stump-like hut, slash at the set of 9 bushes just north of the hut.

Fall into the hole that appears to enter a room with a Piece of Heart. Collect it and then jump to the lower level toward the south. Exit through the door to the left. In the next room is a thief who tells Link that one of their ex-members is by the entrance to the desert. Exit the thief's hut through the door to the south.

Having returned to the Lost Woods, travel north through the left log.

Slash through the bushes to the left to collect the Mushroom. This will later be used to obtain Magic Powder. For now, there are no other tasks that can be completed in the Lost Woods, though Link will return later in the game. Exit the woods the same way Link entered.

Kakariko Village - Main

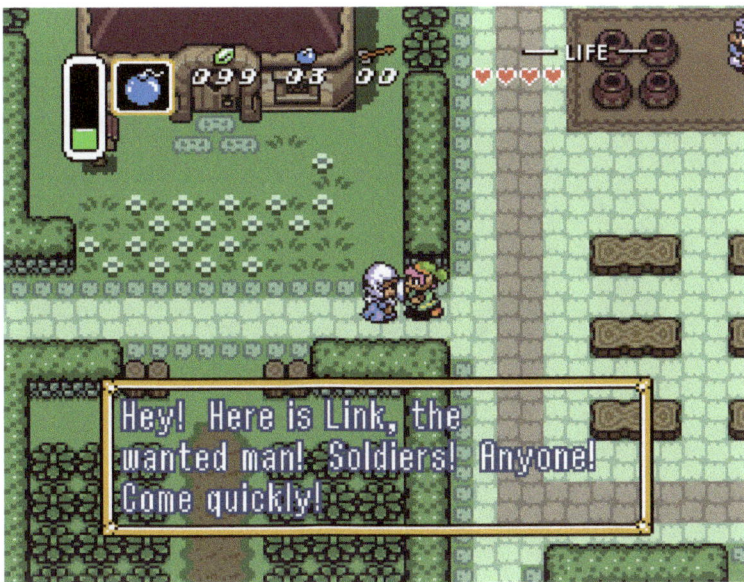

Next, travel through the gate to the south to enter Kakariko Village. Be careful if you travel through the middle of town. Some villagers will recognize Link as a wanted man. If this happens, a Green Spea Soldier will pursue Link until the soldier has been defeated or until Link enters a building.

Head directly to the northwest section of town to find a cave beside a well. Enter the well by jumping into it from the higher ledge.

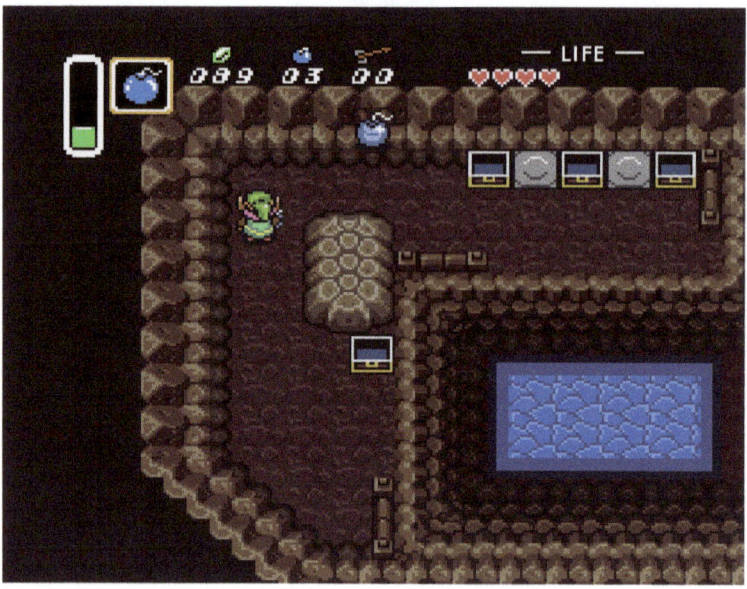

Open the four treasure chests and break the pots to find three Bombs, three Red Rupees, and two Blue Rupees. Next, locate the crack on the Northern wall just slightly left of the 3 treasure chests. Place a Bomb beside it to open a hole in the wall. Bombs will damage Link if he stands too close, so make sure to move out of the way.

Travel through the wall to a room filled with 4 pots and a treasure chest. The pots contain to Blue Rupees and two hearts. The chest at the end of the room contains a Piece of Heart. Exit the cave by returning to the first room and jumping down into the water. Travel right to find the exit door.

In the northern section of town is a hut with a green roof. The man inside tells Link that the house used to be a hangout for thieves. Their leader's name was Blind and he hated bright light. Take the stairwell down to the basement.

The room contains four chests, each holding a single Red Rupee. To acquire all 4, worth 80 Rupees in total, the blocks need to be pushed in a specific order.

First, push the second block from the left down. Repeat this same movement with the block second from the right. Push the block in front of the treasure chest second from the right to the left. The block slightly to the left above that same treasure chest should now be pushed down. Just above and to the right of the second treasure chest from the left is another block that can now be moved. Push it right. From that same treasure chest, the block below and slightly to the right must be pushed downwards. Finally, the block directly below the same treasure chest can't be moved to the left. At this point, all of the treasure chests can be opened.

If a mistake is made, simply exit the basement and return. The blocks will be back in their original positions. **The room can even be repeated an infinite number of times** to acquire Rupees since the chests reset every time the room is exited.

Look closely at the northern wall of the basement. there is a crack in the wall that can be opened using a Bomb. Enter the opened wall to find 6 pots with 6 Blue Rupees and a treasure chest containing another Piece of Heart.

Exit the hut with the green roof and head down the stairs to the south, to the center of town. Find the merchant sitting on a carpet. He will sell Link a Magic Bottle for 100 Rupees. If Link does not have enough money, return to the basement of the hut with the green roof and collect more from the treasure chests.

Next, head to the southwest section of town to find a small building without any windows or doors. Place a Bomb directly in front of it to open an entrance. Inside are two Rats and eight pots. Break the pots to restock Bombs, Arrows, and Rupees. This hut can be repeated an infinite amount of times by exiting and reentering.

Next, head to the Kakariko Inn, a large blue hut on the southern side of town. Travel right from the small hut, past the Kakariko Village Shop to find the inn. Instead of entering from the front door, there is a secret door hidden between a break in the bushes behind the Kakariko Inn.

Walk into the back of the building to enter the behind the bar area of the inn. Break the pots and open the treasure chest to collect a Magic Bottle.

The last item to acquire in Kakariko Village is the Bug Catching Net. Exit the Kakariko Inn and enter the building directly to the north. A boy is in bed, sick with a cold caused by the evil air coming from the mountain. He will allow Link to borrow his Bug-Catching Net while the boy is ill.

Kakariko Village - South

Now that all of the tasks in the main section of Kakariko Village have been completed, travel through the southern gate located in the southeast section of the village. To the left and is a house, home to the Quarreling Brothers.

Inside, use a Bomb to open the crack in the left wall.

From the second room in the house, exit through the southern door. Talk to the woman in pink to begin the 15 Second Game. The purpose is to complete a maze in fifteen seconds to win a Piece of Heart.

To beat the game, slash the five bushes northward. At the end of the five bushes, follow the path left. Next, slash three more bushes and reach the sign in the middle of the maze. The portion of the fence directly south of the sign can be jumped over. Reach the man at the end of the maze to collect the Piece of Heart. If Link fails to beat the maze within the time limit, simply re enter the house and talk to the woman in pink again. By this point, if all of the other Pieces of Heart mentioned earlier in the guide have been collected, Link's total Heart count will increase to five.

Magic Powder

It is now time to the Mushroom in for Magic Powder. Link will need to head to the Magic Shop located outside of Kakariko Village. Green Sword Soldiers, Blue Sword Soldiers, Blue Archers, a Sand Crab, and a Buzz Blob patrol the path. Exit the village by traveling through the northern gate. Walk right, past the Sanctuary and the Hyrulian Cemetery. Travel down one screen and cross the bridge. Then travel back up one screen. The shop is located north of the cliff and to the right.

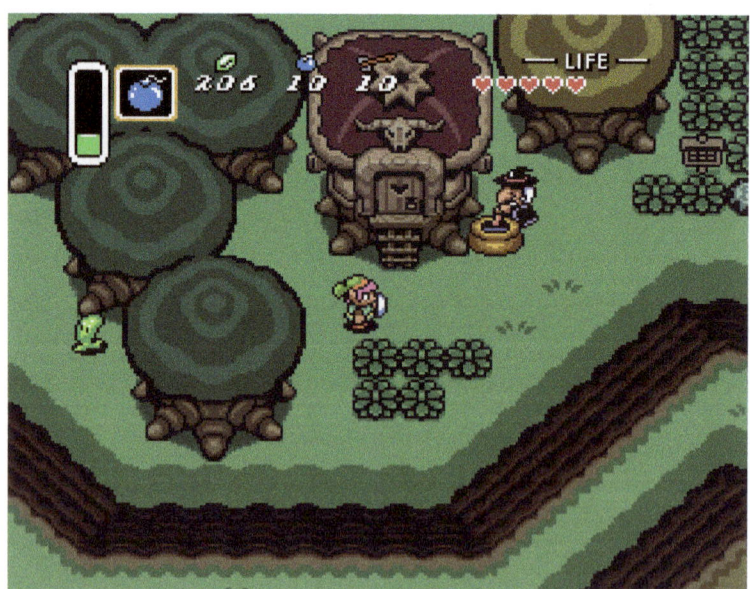

Find Syrup, the shopkeeper, stirring a cauldron of her Magic Shop. Equip the Mushroom and give it to Syrup to return for "something good". Simply exit the current screen by walking left, then return to the Magic Shop.

Enter the shop and collect the Magic Powder located in a bag next to the Hooded Shopkeeper. Magic powder can be used on enemies and objects to cause unique things to happen. consider purchasing a blue potion, if Link has enough Rupees. This will restore both Health and Magic, but will require one empty Magic Bottle to be stored in.

There are a few other items, such as two more Pieces of Heart and the Ice Rod, that Link now has access to. However, they are unnecessary for the next dungeon and out of the way. Instead, these should be collected after Eastern Palace.

Finding Sahasrahla (Optional)

The entire Sahasrahla quest can be ignored by going directly to the Eastern Palace. However, finding Sahasrahla will make the palace easier to find by marking it on the overworld map.

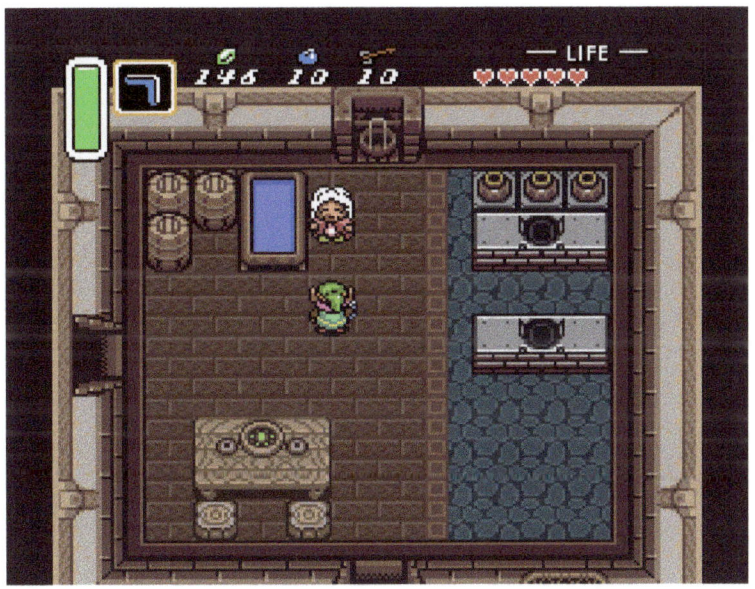

The X currently marked on the overworld map is Sahasrahla's house, the Kakariko Village elder. While his wife is home, he is not. By speaking to the wife, Link will discover that Sahasrahla has vanished. The wife also tells Link the legend of the Master Sword and encourages him to speak to more people in the village.

Outside of the Kakariko Village Shop, on the southern section in the main area of town, is Sahasrahla's Grandson. He knows where his grandfather is and will mark the location on Link's overworld map.

Travel east, past the Sanctuary and Hyrulian Cemetery. Follow the path down, across the bridge, and down another screen. The environment will now become desert-like and filled with Octoroks. Continue south for one more screen and then follow the path to the east, marked by decorative columns. Walk north through the opening between two cliffs to reach the Eastern Palace Compound. Continue north, up the stairs, until Link reaches a house one ground level lower. Jump down and enter the building to locate Sahasrahla.

Talk to Sahasrahla and he will tell Link the location of the three pendants and the Master Sword. Link's first quest is to find the green Pendant of Courage located within the Eastern Palace.

Eastern Palace Compound

If the optional Sahasrahla quest was not completed, Link can go directly to the Eastern Palace Compound from Kakariko Village. Leave the village through the northern gate and travel right. Travel east, past the Sanctuary and Hyrulian Cemetery. Follow the path down, across the bridge, and down another screen. The environment will now become desert-like and filled with Octoroks. Continue south for one more screen and then follow the path to the east, marked by decorative columns. Walk north through the opening between two cliffs to reach the Eastern Palace Compound.

Go up the main stairwell to the compound. Travel north, avoiding or defeating the Octoroks between the bird head statues.

Walk right after going between to higher cliffs to find an Armos blocking the path. Avoid him by luring him away or defeat him. Continue right and south.

To the right of the bird head statue is a gap in the railing. Jump down using the gap to avoid two more Armos enemies.

Continue traveling northeast, up three more sets of stairs and past three more Amos enemies and one Blue Sword Soldier to enter Eastern Palace.

Entering Eastern Palace

In the first room of Eastern Palace is a single pot directly to the north. Lift up it up to expose a switch. When stepped on, this will open the door nearest to the pot. Enter the newly opened door.

Avoid or defeat the Popos in this room. The floor has a slightly raised section that acts as a switch to open another door. Step on the switch and continue through the newly opened door.

In the next room, use the stairs or jump down to reach the lower level. Follow the hallway North, carefully avoiding the Balls. After reaching the hole where the Balls spawn, turn left and follow the hallway. Travel up the stairs and across a narrow walkway to reach four pots and one treasure chest. The treasure chest contains 100 Rupees and the pots contain Rupees of smaller values.

Return across the narrow walkway and down the stairs, back towards the spawning point of the blobs. Take the stairs northwards and enter the door to the upper floor of the main room of the dungeon.

Eastern Palace Dungeon Map (Optional)

Players familiar with the game or those strictly following this guide are not required to obtain a Dungeon Map. However, the Dungeon Map has great value for players who wish to complete the palace with little or no help. It allows Link to view a map of the areas inside the palace. Skip this section if you do not wish to obtain the Dungeon Map.

Follow the pathway to the right to find a statue and two pots. In the corner by the two pots, there's a tile with a raised circle (you can tell by the shadow it has). This is a hidden switch. Step on it to open the door.

Avoid or defeat the Popos and Blue Stalfos in this room. Enter the door to the north on the right side of the room.

The next room contains five pots and a Bubble. Lift the pot in the center of the room to reveal a switch. Step on the switch to open a door on the south side of the room.

Collect the Dungeon Map from the treasure chest, but be careful not to fall down to the floor below. After the Dungeon Map has been collected, jump to the floor below, travel up the stairs, and exit through the door to the left.

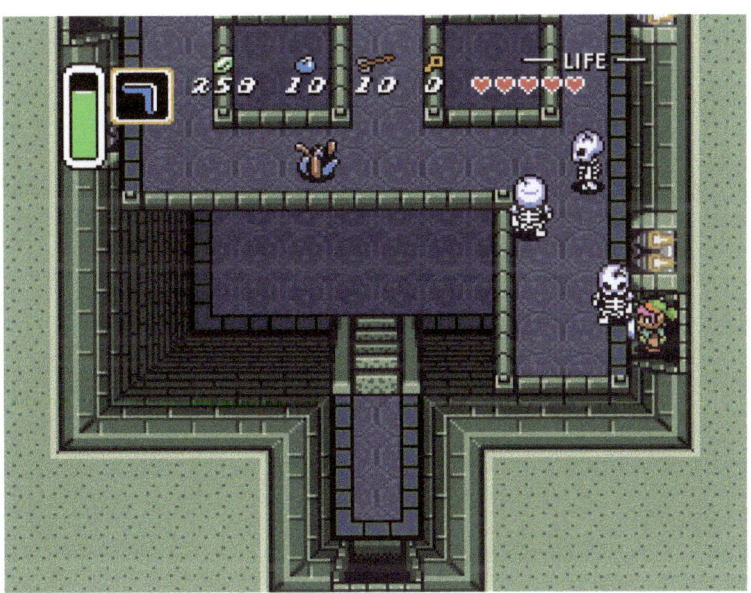

Travel through the room from earlier with Popos and Blue Stalfos. Exit through the door to the left to return to the upper floor of the main room of the dungeon.

Eastern Palace Dungeon Compass

From the upper floor of the main room of the dungeon, travel left to find a statue and two pots. The tile behind the pots is a hidden switch to open the door. Lift the pot and step on the switch. Travel left, through the door.

Avoid or defeat the Blue Stalfos, while traveling south and to the left. Enter the open door.

Now in a room filled with bones, prepare for a small fight. Lift up the pot and the center of the room and for blue stealth us will appear. They can be defeated in the normal manner, but the easiest method is to throw pots at them. One hit with the pot will defeat one Blue Stalfos. There are five pots available in the room, so aim carefully.

Once the Blue Stalfos have been defeated and the door opens, enter the room to the north and collect the compass from the treasure chest.

Follow the stairs down and through the door to the right. Continue right, through another door to enter the lower floor of the main room of the dungeon.

The Bow

For now, avoid the Green Eyegores as well as the Blue Stalfos and ignore the large treasure chest in the middle of the room. Travel through the door to the right.

The next room will be the floor beneath the room with Popos and Blue Stalfos from earlier. Walk south, up the stairs, through an open door.

The darkened room contains to Anti-Fairies that can be seen and two Popos that are hidden in the shadows. A raised tile on the right side of the room acts as a switch. Once stepped on, it will open a door on the right side of the room. Enter the newly opened door.

Several Blue Stalfos patrol the next room. Avoid or defeat them, while traveling right into the north. A Small Key is hidden underneath a pot in that corner of the room. Collect it, then exit back through the door to the left.

Back in the room with the two Anti-Fairies and two Popos, travel to the left side of the room. Open the locked door with the Small Key.

In the next room, follow the narrow hallway left and through the next doorway.

This room contains two Popos, two Blue Stalfos, four Anti-Fairies, and a Green Eyegore. When Link steps too close to the Green Eyegore, the enemy will awaken and begin its attack. The easiest way to complete this room is to carefully defeat the two Blue Stalfos and the two Popos before engaging the Green Eyegore.

Defeating the Green Eyegore will require eight sword slashes. The easiest option to defeat the Green Eyegore is to throw a pot at it while it awakens. One pot will instantly defeat the enemy.

Once the Green Eyegore has been defeated, the four Anti-Fairies will begin to bounce around the room. Lift the pot that they were previously protecting and step on the switch. A treasure chest will appear, containing the Big Key. Open the door to the north and travel through it.

This is the lower floor of the room filled with Blue Stalfos that Link previously visited. Push the block on the right side to continue through the hallway. Travel right to re-enter the lower floor of the main room of the dungeon.

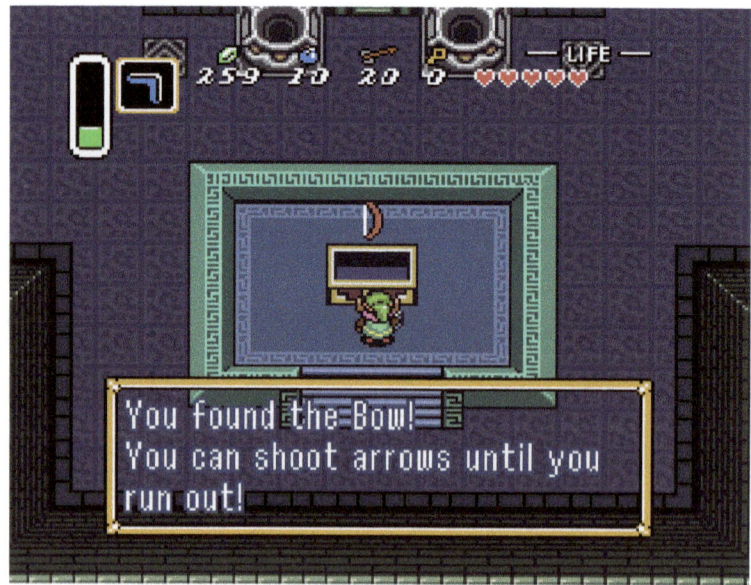

Again, avoid the Green Eyegores and avoid or defeat the Blue Stalfos. Use the big key to open the large treasure chest in the center of the room. This will contain the Bow.

As soon as Link receives the Bow, Grey Stalfos will drop from the ceilings. Avoid or defeat them while heading north to the door leading to the Boss Room.

Finding Eastern Palace Boss Room

Before entering the locked door, it is worthwhile to collect some Fairies. Fairies can be used to heal Life or revive Link. From the platform in front of the door to the Boss Room, drop down and to one of the large white pots.

Link will fall into a room containing two fairies. Use the Bug-Catching Net to capture them. They will be stored in a Magic Bottle (one Fairy per bottle). Use one of the portals located to the left and right of the room to exit back to the lower floor of the main room of the dungeon.

Enter the locked door to find a darkened room filled with Popos and two Green Eyegores. There are three torches in the room that can be lit using the Lamp (north, right, and left). Defeat the Green Eyegore to the right to obtain a small key.

It is optional to travel through the open door to the north on the right side of the room. This room contains two Anti-Fairies and 18 Blue Rupees. After collecting the Rupees, exit the room to the south.

From the room containing the Two Green Eyegore and Popos, walk left and north. Enter the locked door.

Two Anti-Fairies bounce around the room. Lift the bottom, left pot and step on the switch to open the door on the left side of the room.

Three Green Eyegores await in the next room. Defeat them then step on the southern floor tile switch to open a door to the left.

In this room, Balls spawn from many points. Avoid them and step on the top left floor tile switch to open another door to the left.

Defeat the two Blue Stalfos before engaging the Red Eyegore. Hit its open eye with two arrows to defeat it. This will cause the door to the north to open.

Continue north to a room with six pots, six Popos, and two Red Eyegores. With correct timing, it is possible to defeat all of the Popos using a well placed Spin Attack. Defeat the Popos before defeating the Red Eyegores, then exit through the newly opened door to the north. This door leads directly to the Boss Room.

BOSS BATTLE Six Armos Knights

Unlike most Boss Rooms in The Legend of Zelda franchise, the Eastern Palace Boss Room contains 6 mini bosses. These Armos Statues will come to life as Armos Knights and begin jumping around the room.

First, the Armos Knights will form a circle, traveling clockwise. Next, they will line up on the North side of the room and move towards the South. Each Armos Knight will take sixteen sword hits or three Arrows to be defeated.

The easiest method to defeat them is to stand in the right corner to the South. Look north and shoot the Armos Knights with the Bow as they travel towards Link. When Link has defeated all but one of the Armos Knights, the last Armos Knight will turn red and begin attacking Link. Move quickly around the room, avoiding the Red Armos Knight. Defeat him with a few Arrows or several sword slashes.

After all of the Armos Knights have been defeated, collect the Hearts Container and the Pendant of Courage. Obtaining the Pendant of Courage will transport link outside of the dungeon.

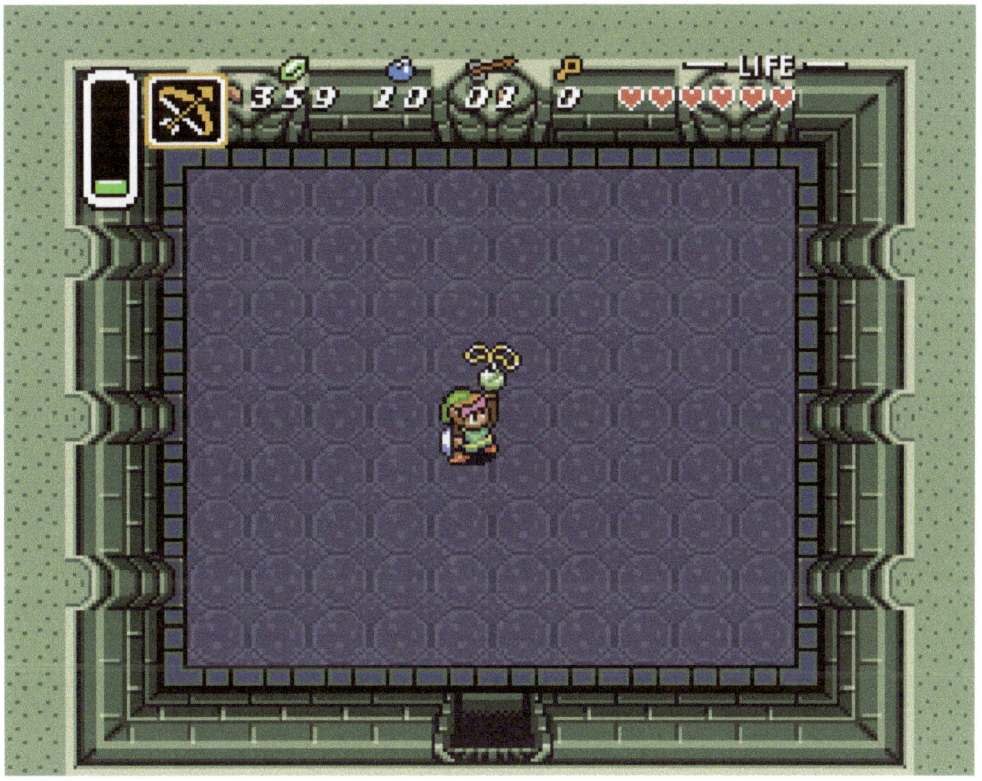

Desert Palace

Total Life   6

Heart Pieces   4 /24

The next Pendant of Virtue, the Pendant of Power, is hidden inside of Desert Palace. IN order to enter the palace and collect the pendant, Link must obtain the Pegasus Boots.

The Pegasus Boots

With the Pendant of Courage now in Link's possession, Link must visit Sahasrahla inside of the Eastern Palace Compound. From the entrance to the Palace, travel left until reaching a small hut.

Once inside, speak to Sahasrahla to receive the Pegasus Boots. With these, Link now gains the ability to use a dash attack. This attack also allows Link to run in a straight path. Running into certain stationary objects, such as trees, may cause items to appear (hearts, rupees, etc.). Sahasrahla also encourages Link to seek a mysterious on the eastern side of Lake Hylia.

Behind Sahasrahla and the three pots is a cracked wall. Use either a Bomb or the Pegasus Boots to break through the wall. Open the treasure chests to collect a total of 100 Rupees and three Bombs. Exit the hut.

The Book of Mudora

The Overworld map now only marks the two remaining Pendants of Virtue and the Master Sword. Although the blue Pendant of Power in Desert Palace is the next one be collected, the Book of Mudora is needed to enter the Palace. To obtain the Book of Mudora, Link will need to return to Kakariko Village.

To return to Kakariko Village, exit the Eastern Palace Compound by traveling south. Once in the Overworld, follow the path left between the columns, north through a desert area filled with Octoroks, north and to the right to find the bridge, cross the bridge to the left, follow the path north, and the continue to follow the path past the Hyrule Cemetery and Sanctuary.

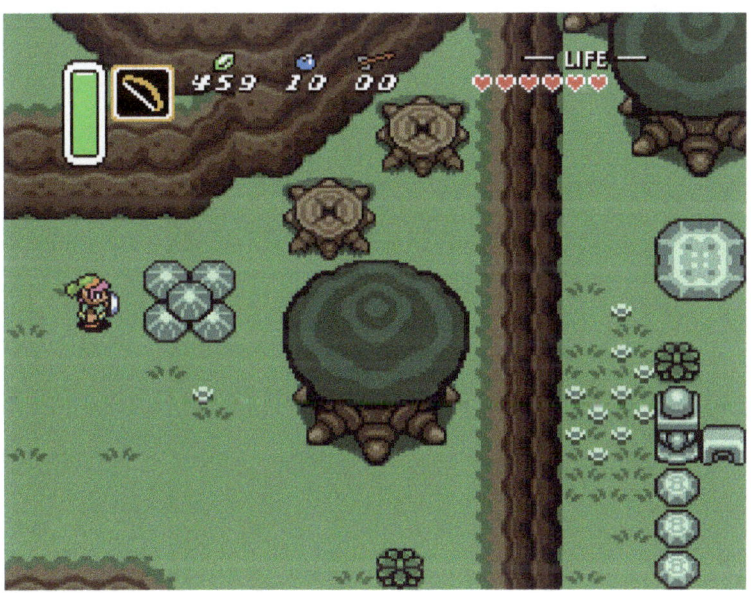

On the screen directly to the left of the Sanctuary, travel north, then head right to find a stack of five boulders. Use the attack to clear the boulders and enter the hole.

Open the treasure chest inside to find a piece of hearts. Exit the hole and return to the path. Travel left one more screen to find the Kakariko Village gate to the south.

Continue south through the village and through the southern gate to enter the southern section of Kakariko Village. This is the same area of town with the Quarreling Brothers.

Enter the first hut to the left to find a room filled with bookshelves. On top of the closest book shelf to the left is a loan book. Use Link's newly-acquired dash attack to knock the book off of the shelf. Collect the book off of the ground to obtain the Book of Mudora.

The Great Swamp

Exit the Hutt and travel South. When the screen dead ends, follow the pathway right. Continue to follow the path right. First it will head south, then north. Several Blue and Green Sword Soldiers patrol the area. Defeat or avoid them. Eventually, arrive back at Link's House.

Next, travel south to enter Great Swamp. Follow the cliff side to the right until Link comes across a crack in the wall. Use a Bomb to blow a hole in the cliff side and enter the cave.

Inside is a Faerie Spring. Talk to the Faerie to heal Link back to full health. Exit the cave and continue south, past the Green Archers.

From the next screen, travel left to reach the Swamp Ruins. Link will return here later in his quests to further explore the ruins. For now, there is a Piece of Heart that can be collected.

Enter the Swamp Ruins and push the blocks on the far right and the far left up. Next, move the center block either to the right or to the left to gain access to the treasure chest. Open the treasure chest to collect three Bombs. Exit the Swamp Ruins and reenter them to reset the blocks.

 Push the center block up. Then, push the right block to the right or the left block to the left. This should clear a pathway for Link to walk behind the treasure chest and enter the open door.

In the next room, and Anti-Fairy bounces off of the wall. On the northern wall, pull the lever on the right. This should unblock the water and allow it to flow south. Exit the Swamp Ruins. To the left of the ruins is a Piece of Heart in a puddle of water. Collect it.

Along with the Piece of Heart, a Fish will jump out of the puddles to the right and left. Link can pick up Fish and carry them around. If Link is attacked, he will drop the Fish. Dropped Fish can be picked back up. Fish can be released into a body of water for a single Red Rupee.

Alternatively, Fish can be taken to the Bottle Merchant in Kakariko Village and exchanged for Rupees, Bombs, Arrows, and a large Magic Jar.

Travel right two screens from the Swamp Ruins and locate a crack in the cliff side to the north. Use a bomb to open it and enter the cave.

Inside, use Arrows or throw Bombs to defeat the four Mini-Moldorms. Avoid falling in the pits. Another method is to walk in the narrow space between the wall and the pits and slash the Mini-Moldorms. Once the enemies have been defeated, a door on the north side of the room will open.

Speak to the Thief to collect 300 Rupees. Open the treasure chests for more Rupees, as well as Bombs and Arrows. Exit the cave.

The Ice Rod

Head east and follow the edge of Lake Hylia until the pathway dead ends at a cave entrance near a severed bridge.

Enter the cave and use a bomb to open the crack on the northern wall. Collect Fairies if they are needed, but save one empty Magic Bottle. Hidden inside of the statue is a Good Bee. Good Bees can be released to defeat all onscreen enemies. Dash attack into the statue to find the Bee, then use the Bug-Catching Net to collect it.

Once outside of the cave, open the crack on the cliff side to the left of the entryway you just used before. Enter the passageway and continue north.

Open the treasure chest to obtain the Ice Rod.

The Desert of Mystery

It is now time to enter the Desert of Mystery, located and the southwest section of the overworld. Exit the cave and follow the shore of Lake Hylia back to the left, towards the Great Swamp. Continue traveling left, past the Swamp Ruins and into a narrow mountainous region. Continue traveling left to reach the Desert of Mystery.

Where the ground begins to transition from grass to sand, look in the cliff wall to the north for a cave entrance. Inside is a Faerie Spring. Talk to the Faerie to recover health.

Continue to follow the narrow pathway into the Desert of Mystery. Travel north to find a cave located in the right corner.

Enter the cave and follow the hallway into a room with a man. On the Southern Wall, use a bomb to blow open the crack.

Inside, collect another Piece of Heart from the treasure chest, then exit the cave.

Entering Desert Palace

With the Book of Mudora in hand, the Desert Palace can now be opened. Travel left to the palace's entrance. Using the Book of Mudora, read the stone block in the center of the three statues. Link will sing and the three statues will move, opening the entrance to the Desert Palace. Walk up the steps to enter the palace.

Desert Palace has many different corridors and rooms, some of which are optional. This guide will ignore rooms in Desert Palace that contain no importance.

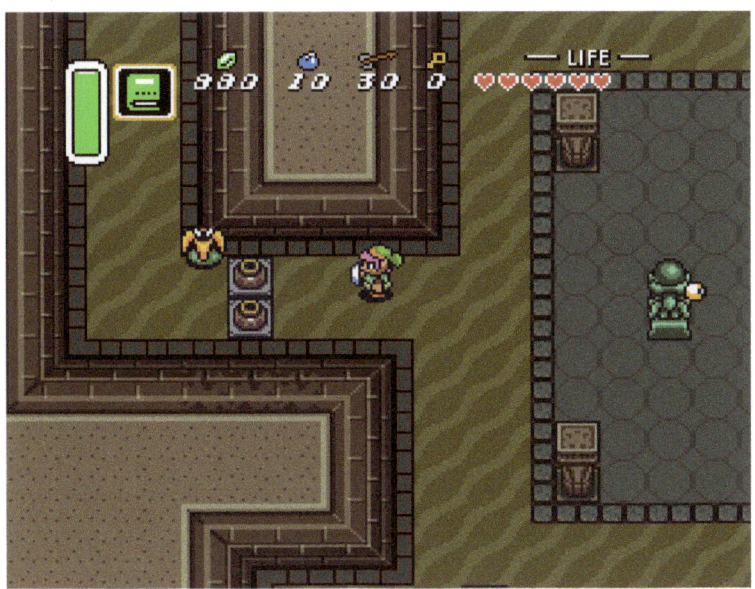

The main room in the palace has several Leevers, both purple and green, as well as a Beamos. Travel north towards the Beamos, then take the path to the left blocked by two pots. Break one or both of the pots to follow the path north. Beware of the Red Devalant hiding towards the end of the path.

Desert Palace Dungeon Map (Optional)

Continue through the door just north of where the pathway ends. Defeat or avoid the two Green Eyegores, the purple Leever, and the Green Lever. On the north side of the room, pick up the center pot to reveal a button. Step on the button and a treasure chest will appear to the south. Open the chest to find the Dungeon Map. Exit the room the way it was entered; exit through the door to the left.

The Power Glove

Travel left and enter the first door.

Avoid the Beamos. Use the dash attack to knock the small key off of the torch. Pick it up and exit the room.

Travel to the far right of the room, then head south to find a locked door to the right. Enter the door by using the small key.

Defeat all of the Popos in the room while avoiding the Beamos. Open the treasure chest to obtain the Dungeon Compass (optional). Once all of the Popos have been defeated, the door to the north will open and Link may travel through it.

Wall Turrets on the sides of the room shoot Balls at Link. Avoid the Balls to reach a treasure chest. Collect the Big Key and return to the main room of the palace.

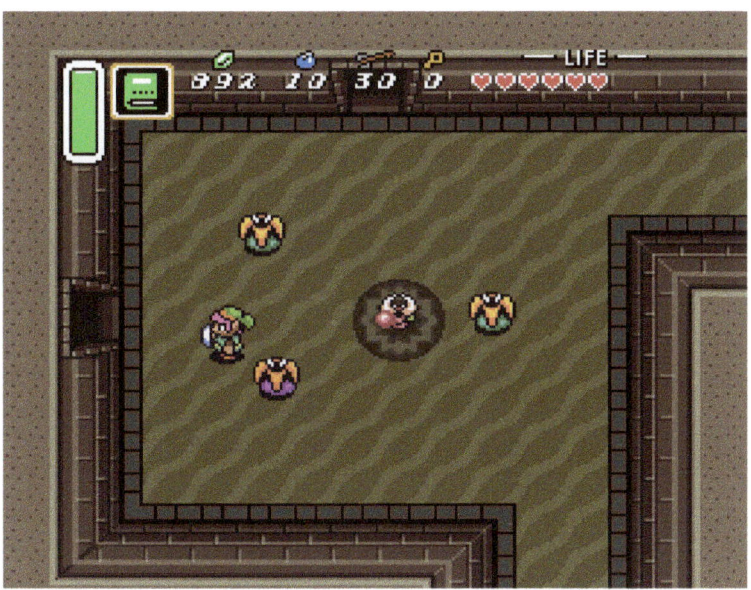

Head back towards the room with the first small key by traveling north and the following the hallway left. Pass the room with the small key and enter the room to the left and slightly south.

A Beamos sits in the center of the room, surrounded by pots. A switch to open the doors is hidden beneath the pot located to the left and north. Avoid the Beamos, step on the switch, and enter the door to the north.

Open the large treasure chest to receive the Power Glove.

Finding Desert Palace Boss Room

Return to the main room of the palace. Keep to the left and travel south to find an opened door. Enter the room.

Inside waits another Beamos. If necessary, the northern door leads to a Faerie Springs. To unlock it, go to the left group of four blocks. Move the second block from the right up or down. Exit the palace through the door to the south.

Once outside, follow the path south to find a Piece of Heart.

Next, travel north and follow the cliff wall to the right. Behind the original entrance to the Desert Palace is a entrance blocked by four boulders. Having now acquired the Power Glove, Link can lift these boulders as easily as pots. Clear a path to the entrance and enter the second half of the palace.

Another Beamos patrols this room. On the right side of the room is a set of three blocks. Move the southern one in any direction to open the door to the north. Enter the newly opened door.

At first glance, this room appears to be empty of enemies. However, twenty Flying Tiles will rise from the ground and attack Link. Either wait at the entrance for the Flying Tiles to destroy themselves, or avoid them. Lift the southern pot on the left side of the room to obtain a small key. Unlock the door to the north by using the small key.

Follow the hallway south and through the open door. This next room is filled with Popos and a Beamos. Defeat all of the Popo to unlock the doors. Enter the door to the right.

Follow the hallway north, past several Popos and two Beamos to reach four pots. Life the second pot from the right to obtain an small key. Continue north, past another Beamos, and open the door.

Again, twenty Flying Tiles hide on the floor. Avoid them and collect the key from the northern pot on the right. Open the door to the north and enter.

Follow the room to the left and defeat the Red Eyegore. Use the Lamp to light the four torches. The left wall will move, revealing the entrance to the Boss Room.

BOSS BATTLE Three Lanmolas

The boss of Desert Palace is a group of three Lanmolas, giant sand worms. They are invincible everywhere except for their heads. Link can use the Fighter's Sword, Bow, or Bombs to defeat the Lanmolas, but the Ice Rod does the most damage. However, much like Bombs and Arrows, the Ice Rod requires more accuracy and timing than the sword. Each of Lanmolas will require six sword slashes to be defeated

Lanmolas constantly burrow underground before and after attacking. The ground will turn red and rocky whenever they are near the surface, allowing Link to detect the location of a Lanmola. They attack by shooting four rocks diagonally in each direction every time they surface from the ground. Touching a Lanmola will also cause damage.

 Once there is one Lanmola left, its pattern of attack will change. When it returns from underground, it will shoot eight rocks both straight and diagonally. Continue to avoid the rocks and attack the Lanmola's head until it has been defeated.

Collect the Piece of Heart and the Pendant of Power. Link will be transported outside the second portion of the Desert Palace.

Tower of Hera

Total Life   8

Heart Pieces   8/24

Inside the Tower of Hera is the final pendant, the Pendant of Wisdom. After collecting a few items from around the overworld, Link will need to travel to the top of Death Mountain to find the Tower of Hera. Once inside the tower, he must defeat the boss on the top floor to obtain the pendant.

The next object Link will need to collect are the Zora Flippers. In order to purchase these, Link will need 500 rupees.

Zora's Flippers

From Desert Palace, travel south across the Desert of Mystery. Walk right, towards the Great Swamp. When the desert terrain turn to grass, look for two larger boulders to the south. Lift up the southernmost boulder to expose a hole in the ground.

Enter the hole to find a Thief surrounded by 10 pots. Each of the pots holds one blue rupee.

Exit the cave and continue right, towards the Swamp Ruins. Follow the edge of the cliff north until Link finds another large boulder. Pick it up to remove it from the path and continue north. At the area containing Green Sword Soldiers and two patches of grass (with six grasses per patch), travel slightly left while continuing northward. To the right, a narrow path is blocked by grass. Slash the grass and walk right.

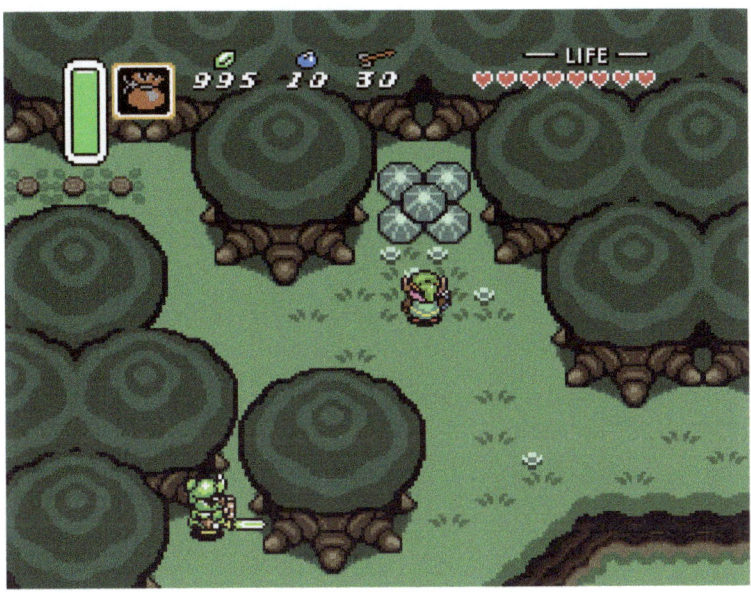

Use the dash attack to clear the pile of five boulders. In the cave below is a Faerie Spring.

Continue traveling right, reaching Link's House. Now, walk north to Hyrule Castle. Once at the castle, travel right and throw the rock out of the way to clear a pathway right.

Continue right until reaching a cliff way. Walk north, towards the Potion Shop. Just east of the Potion Shop is another boulder for Link to pick up.

Clear the boulder and follow the pathway right and south. Three piles of boulders block a path near a stairwell. Use the dash attack to clear the path and travel right, up an incline and into an area where the grass has turned brown.

Continue traveling north. The lightest colored water in this area is shallow enough for Link to walk on. The river is filled with River Zora. Watch for the spiraling water that warns when one will surface. Follow the river north until the forest edge prevents any more travel.

The river continues to the right, with the light colored water splitting into four paths. Take the southern water path, heading right.

When Link arrives at the Waterfall, King Zora will emerge from the water and offer to sell Link the Zora Flippers. Pay the price of 500 rupees to obtain the Zora flippers, allowing Link to swim in deep water. King Zora will also grant Link access to all of the Zora Waterways in Hyrul

e.

From King Zora, swim south to find another waterfall. Jump down it and swim left to find a Piece of Heart on a small section of land.

Return to the river, down the same slope Link used to get onto the land and down the waterfall to the south. Follow the river left and to the south until patches of brown grass appear.

The Mysterious Pond (Optional)

Swim left into the water. To the north is another waterfall. Swim into the center of it to find a hidden cave containing a Mysterious Pond.

The Mysterious Pond is guarded by a fairy. If Link throws an item into the pond, she will return it to him. If Link throws in certain items, they can be upgraded. The Boomerang becomes the Magical Boomerang (now able to fly faster and able to cut down bushes). The Fighter's Shield becomes the Fire Shield (protects against small fireballs). An empty Magic Bottle will return filled with Medicine of Magic. Upgrade the shield and Boomerang and exit the cave.

The Pond of Happiness (Optional)

From the Mysterious Pond, swim south to a swirling section of water. Though it looks like an area where a River Zora will emerge, this is actually a Zora Waterway. Swimming into it will transport Link to Lake Hylia.

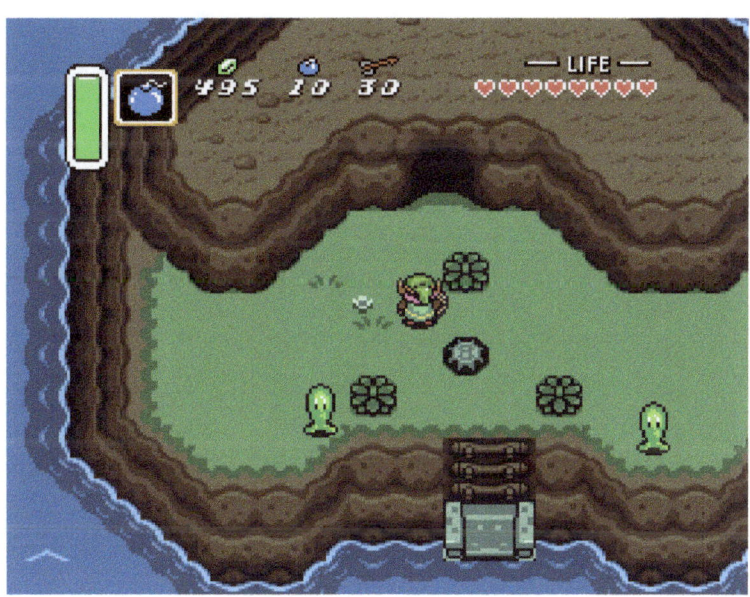

Swim north, onto a small island with a cave. Enter the cave and follow the narrow hallway north.

This is the Pond of Happiness and it allows Link to throw in rupees to upgrade the amount of Bombs or Arrows he can carry. The first few times, Link is allowed to throw in either five or twenty rupees. Walk a few steps away from the pond and return to throw in more rupees until Link has thrown in one hundred rupees. The Queen of Fairies, Venus, will emerge from the water and allow Link to choose between upgrading his Bombs to fifteen or Arrows to thirty five.

After the initial upgrade, Link can return to the pond and throw in twenty five or fifty rupees at a time. Every time a total of 100 rupees have been tossed into the Pond of Happiness, Link will be able to upgrade his Bombs or Arrows by increments of five. The maximum Link can upgrade is to fifty Bombs and seventy Arrows. When Link reaches forty Bombs or 60 Arrows, one hundred rupees will upgrade them by ten instead of five.

On the right wall of the cave is a crack. Use a Bomb to open the wall. Inside is a Faerie Spring.

Outside of the cave, jump into the water on the right side of the island and swim north. Follow the narrow stream of water to Hyrule Castle's bridge. Swim into it to be transported to an area underneath.

Talk to the Camper to obtain a third empty Magic Bottle.

Exit the Camper's area by swimming right. Follow the water back to Lake Hylia. Use the stairs to the right to get back on land. Follow the grass north. Travel left past the Desert Palace Compound and north through the desert area infested with Octoroks. Walk left across the bridge and continue north.

Hyrulian Cemetery (Optional)

Follow the dirt path to the left to reach the Hyrulian Cemetery.

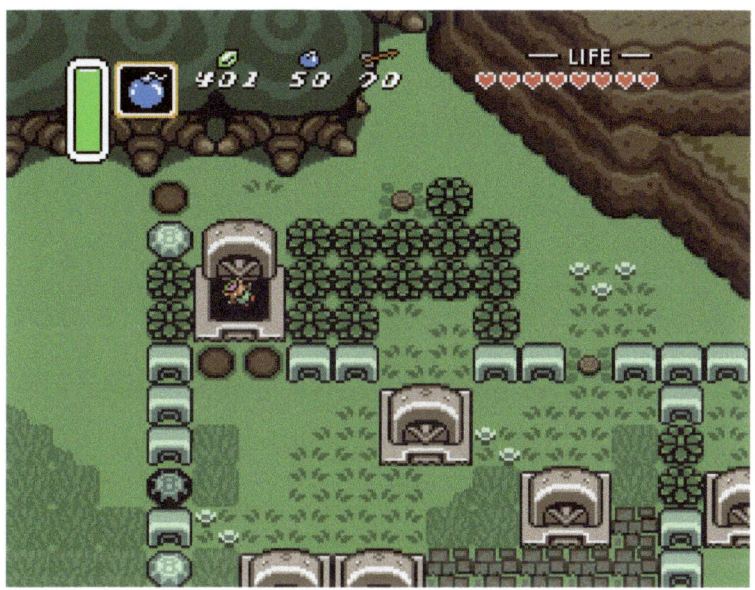

Pushing the gravestone at the very northwest edge of the graveyard opens a hole in the ground. To reach the gravestone, either through the cemetery and defeat or avoid the Spear Knight. Alternatively, travel around the outside of the graveyard fence, then throw the boulders and cut the grass near the gravestone. In order to push the gravestone, two boulders in front of it must be lifted out of the way.

Once inside the hole, Link is back inside the sewers of Hyrule Castle. Travel south and to the left to blast open a cracked hole in the wall. Collect the hearts from the pots and the bombs, arrows, and rupees from the treasure chests. Exit the room and travel north. Move the middle block to open a pathway and travel up the stairs. Like earlier in the game, travel through a room with pots and Rats to reach the room with the levers which open the door.

Now inside the Sanctuary, exit back to the Overworld.

Finding Death Mountain

Travel to the left, past the Sanctuary, then turn north. Continue north, past the Buzz Blobs and Crows. To the right will be a large boulder blocking a cave entrance. Pick up the boulder to clear the path and enter the cave to Death Mountain.

The cave is dark, full of Kesses, and Link has only his Lamp to guide him. Jump down and travel to the right at the first intersection. Shortly, there will be a narrow path to the north. Walk up it to find the Old Man to the right. Speak to him and he will follow Link. Along the way, he will offer advice, directions, and lore.

Travel through the opening behind the Old Man. In this next area, avoid the hole in the earth and travel right. At the far end of the room, the Old Man will direct Link to turn right. Follow the instructions, heading south. Travel through the doorway to exit the cave to reach Death Mountain.

The Magic Mirror

Boulders fall from above and Deadrocks patrol the area. Avoid the enemies and travel to the right. Once Link reaches the open doorway, the Old Man will give him the Magic Mirror. The Magic Mirror can be used to teleport Link between the Light World and the Dark World. If used inside a dungeon, it will teleport Link to the dungeon entrance.

Enter the cave that the Old Man has walked into. Talking to the Old Man will replenish Link's health. At any point, Link can return to this cave to heal.

Death Mountain

Exit the cave and travel right, up the first set of stairs, and continue right. Head north towards a cave entrance. Do not enter the cave, but travel left to find another cave entrance.

Again, do not enter the cave, but walk up the long ladder that's adjacent to he entrance.

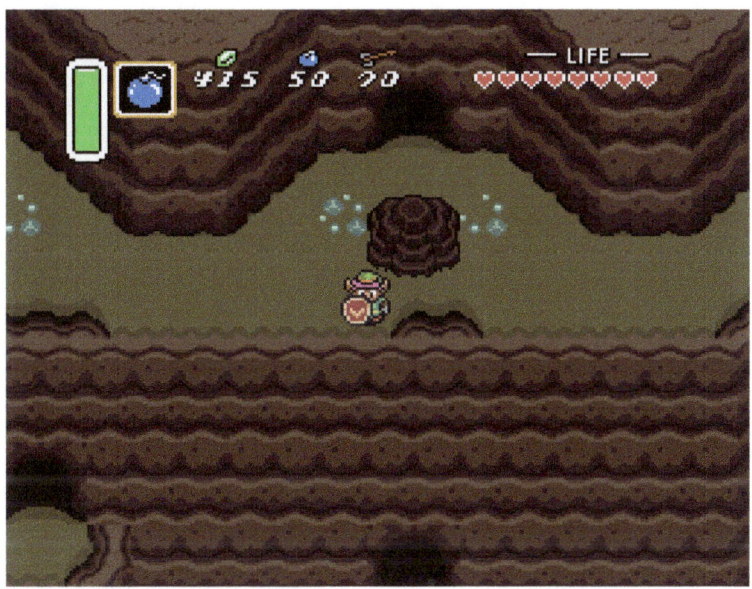

Walk right to find a third cave entrance. Once again, don't enter the cave. Instead, jump down the southern cliffside directly below the third cave entrance. Enter this fourth cave entrance.

Follow the cave northward, up the stairs and through the doorway. Collect the Piece of Heart and then fall through the ground to the south.

Travel right to find a Faerie Spring. Walk left and follow the pathway, past the Mini-Moldorms, to exit the cave. Jump down from the ledge. Continue walking left to long stairwell again.

Travel right, past the third cave from before, to reach a group of three boulders with a warp point in the center. Step onto the warp portal and Link will be teleported to the Dark World.

Once in the Dark World, Link will be transformed into a rabbit. As a rabbit, Link is unable to use weapons and most items.

Travel left to a diamond shape in the ground. Stand on the diamond and use the Magic Mirror.

Back in the Light World, Link is on top of Spectacle Rock. Collect the Piece of Heart.

Jump off of the north side of Spectacle Rock and travel right to reach the Tower of Hera.

Entering Tower of Hera

Once inside the main room of the Tower of Hera, slash the crystal switch and the blue blocks will lower. Walk through the door to the left.

A Blue Stalfos, a Red Stalfos, and a Mini-Moldorm can be avoided or defeated. Either slash the crystal switch or use the Boomerang to obtain the small key. Exit the room.

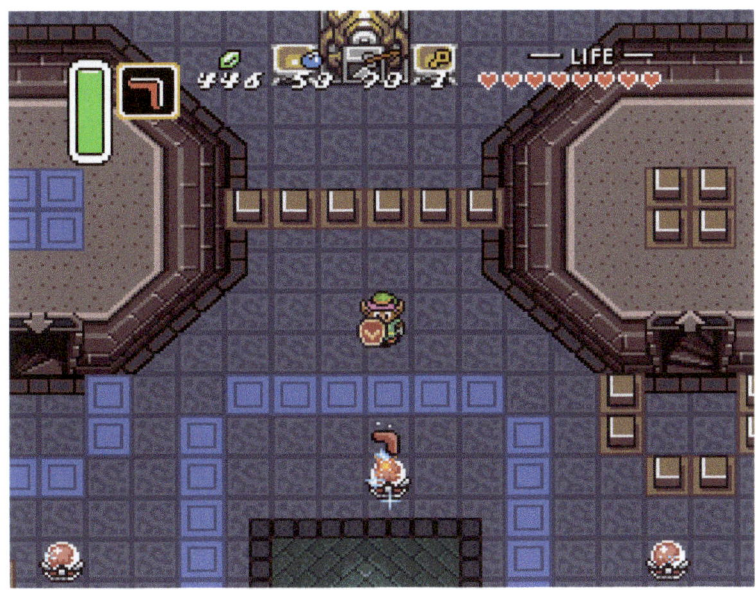

Stand outside of the blue blocks near the tower entrance in the main room of the Tower of Hera and use the Boomerang to hit the crystal switch. The blue blocks will raise and the red blocks will lower.

Travel to the north end of the room. Open the treasure chest to receive the Dungeon Map.

Open the door to the left by using the small key.

This room is filled with twenty Floating Tiles. Avoid them or slash them with the Fighter's Sword until all of them have been exposed. The door to the right will open. Hit the crystal switch to lower the blue blocks and exit the room.

In the next room, hit the crystal switch to lower the red blocks. Avoid or defeat the Mini-Moldorms and exit to the south.

All four torches in the room need to be lit by using the Lamp. This is much easier if the Two Red Stalfos have been defeated first. Once the four torches are lit, a treasure chest will appear. Open it to obtain the Big Key.

Travel back to the previous room with the Mini-Moldorms. Hit the crystal switch to raise the red blocks. Exit to the left and hit the crystal switch to raise the blue blocks. Travel through the door to the north to the main room of the Tower of Hera.

Head to the southern corner to the right, enter the door heading upwards.

Defeat the three Hardhat Beetles without falling through the holes in the floor. Once the enemies have been defeated, exit through the newly opened door to the left.

The two stars on the floor with change the positions of the two holes in the floor. Avoid or defeat the two Hardhat Beetles and use the stars on the floor to clear a path to the door.

Enter the door to the next room. Travel to the right, avoiding or defeating the Hardhat Beetles. Use the stars on the floor if necessary to clear an easier path. Once at the door on the far right side of the room, make sure the crystal switch is red and the blue blocks are raised. If they are not, hit the crystal switch. Enter the doorway and head up.

Walk south, defeating the two Mini-Moldorms trapped between the pots and walls. Walk left and open the treasure chest containing the Dungeon Compass.

The Moon Pearl

Make sure that the star on the floor is lit up to the right of the treasure chest. Walk to the left and travel north to a doorway heading up.

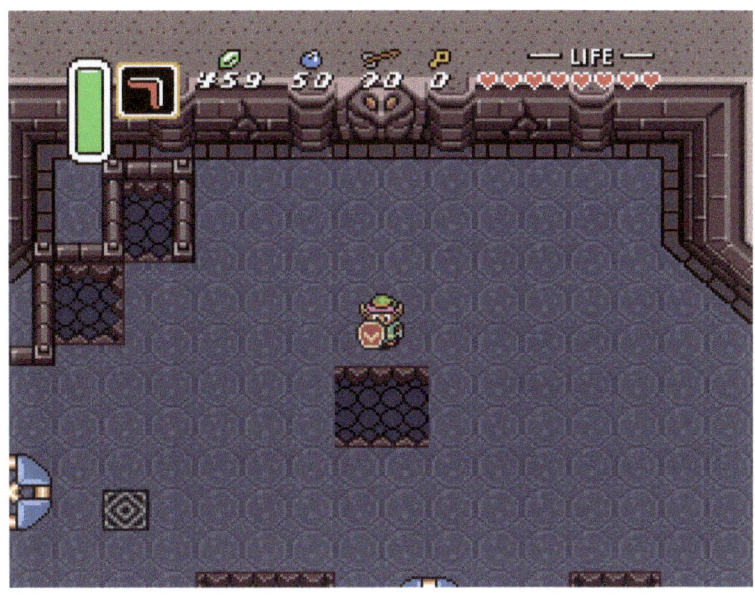

Step onto the star just south of the doorway. Be cautious of the Guruguru Bar that rotates around it. Just north of the center of the room will appear a hole in the floor. Stand to the north of it and jump into it.

Open the large treasure chest to the north to recieve the Moon Pearl. The Moon Pearl allows Link to travel into the Dark World without becoming a rabbit.

Finding Tower of Hera Boss Room

Step on a star to the south and travel back through the door to the north on the left side of the room. Once again in the room with the Guruguru Bar, do not step on the star. Fall into the hole to the left at the north wall of the room.

Link will fall through several pots and floors, finally reaching a Faerie Spring.

Step onto the warp portal to return to the original floor Link fell from. This time, however, the door to the right of the room will be marked with a boss symbol in front of it. The pots just south of the door contain hearts. Link can use these between attempts at the Boss Room.

BOSS BATTLE Moldorm

The Tower of Hera is guarded by Moldorm, a much larger version of the Mini-Moldorms Link has previously battled. Jump into the battle area from the wall at the south of the room.

Moldorm doesn't have a particular attack. Rather, if Moldorm's head touches Link (or Link's sword touches Moldorm's head), Link will lose one heart and will be pushed backwards. If Link falls off of the edge of the battle area, the entire battle will have to be restarted.

The key to defeating Moldorm is patience and perseverance. Use the small wall to the south as a buffer. It is the only place in the battle area where Link will not fall. Choose when to attack wisely.

Defeat Moldorm by slashing its tail with the Fighter's Sword. After five hits, Moldorm will speed up. Hit the tail one more time to defeat it.

Collect the Heart Container, bringing Link's total heart count to nine. Next, pick up the Pendant of Wisdom. With all three collected, Link can now wield the Master Sword. Obtaining the Pendant of Wisdom will transport Link outside of the Tower of Hera.

Hyrule Castle Tower

Total Life   9

Heart Pieces   11.75 /24

With all three Pendants of Virtue collected, Link's next task is to obtain the Master Sword which is located in the Lost Woods. Shortly after Link collects the Master Sword, Agahnim kidnaps Princess Zelda and takes her to the Hyrule Castle Tower. Link must break into Hyrule Castle, climb to the top of the tower, and attempt to defeat Agahnim before the seal of the seven wise men can be broken.

The Master Sword

Now outside of the Tower of Hera, jump south from the ledge. Travel south and to the left to reach the cave entrance near the long stairwell.

Avoid the holes and Keeses in the darkened cave. Follow the cave through two rooms to find a door to the south. Exit through the door to exit Death Mountain.

Walk north and two the left, past the Twin Lumberjacks, to enter the Lost Woods.

Travel south and enter the right log. Next, travel north through the left log.

Follow the path to the left and slash the bushes to enter another log heading northward.

Continue following the path, slashing an area of four bushes and entering another log to the south.

After exiting the log, walk left, passing another log to the south. Enter the log to the far left heading north.

The forest creatures in this area of the Lost Woods will not harm Link. Travel to the north to find a pedestal containing the Master Sword. The Master Sword is twice as strong as the Fighter's Sword, has a longer reach, and can fire a beam attack when Link is at full health. Pull it out of the pedestal and it will trigger a telepathic communication with Sahasrahla.

Now that the Lost woods has been cleared of evil, exit the area through the log to the south. Immediately, Link will receive another telepathic communication. This time, it's from Princess Zelda. Soldiers are entering the Sanctuary!

Ether Medallion

Before rescuing Princess Zelda, Link can obtain the Ether Medallion. Exit the Lost Woods by backtracking the same path Link took to the Master Sword. Travel past the Twin Lumberjacks and enter the cave to Death Mountain.

This time, there will be no Old Man to guide Link. Take the same path the Old Man used the first time Link traveled through the mountain. Climb up Death Mountain and use the warp portal on the top to enter the Dark World.

Due to now having the Moon Pearl, Link will remain in his normal form. Walk into the diamond to the left and use the Magic Mirror to be teleported back to Spectacle Rock in the Light World. Jump off of the north side and travel towards the Tower of Hera.

Walk left, across the bridge to find a large tablet. Use the Book of Mudora in front of it and Link will be granted the Ether Medallion. This medallion if the first of three. When used alongside the Master Sword, the Ether Medallion will freeze a large area, killing weaker enemies and freezing tougher ones.

Return to the Sanctuary

With the Ether Medallion obtained, leave Death Mountain. Once back outside of the cave leading to Death Mountain, travel south and to the right to reach the Sanctuary.

Inside, the Loyal Sage lays wounded on the ground. Talk to him to find out that Zelda has been taken to Hyrule Castle.

Entering Hyrule Castle Tower

Exit the sanctuary and travel left and then south to narrow path to the right which leads to Hyrule Castle.

Follow the castle walls right and to the south to reach the castle courtyard. Follow the stone path to the north to enter Hyrule Castle through its main doors.

Once inside, enter the door on the left.

Travel up the stairs to the south and through the opened doorway to the outside.

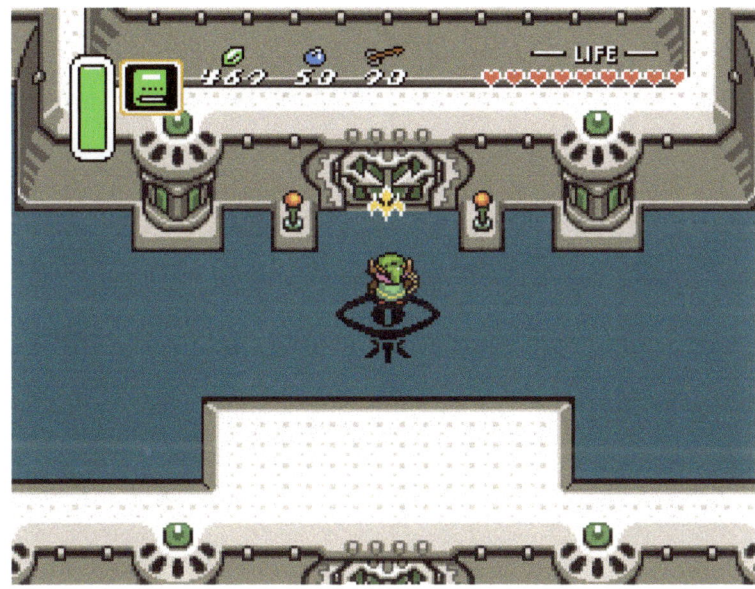

Walk right to find a door blocked by electricity. Slash the barrier with the Master Sword. Once the electricity vanishes, enter Hyrule Castle Tower.

Hyrule Castle Tower

The first room in the tower has no enemies, so travel through the door to the north. This room contains two Gold Ball and Chain Troopers. Defeat them to unlock the door to the right. If Link is at full health, use the barriers in the room to stop the enemies from moving forward while attacking them with the beam attack.

In the next room, two Sword Knights must be defeated. After they have both been defeated, a treasure chest will appear. Collect the small key from the treasure chest and enter the door to the north.

Another Sword Knight and a Chasupa hide in the dark. Follow the red carpet to the left, avoiding or defeating the enemies.

The next room is a maze. Travel north, following the path to the left and then south to find a torch. Light it using the Lamp. Get the small key from the treasure chest to the left.

Walk to the right, to the locked door to the south. If at any point the torch goes out, it can be relit. Unlock the door and travel through.

Although the room is originally lit when Link enters, the lights will quickly fade to darkness. Two Blue Sword Soldiers lurk in the dark of the next room. Defeat or avoid them and travel through the door to the north.

Another dark room awaits. Inside, a Blue Sword Soldier and a Blue Archer patrol. Avoid or defeat them and follow the red carpet through a door to the left.

Walk straight to the left to light a torch in the center of the room. Be careful, as there are several Blue Sword Soldiers within the room. Follow the path to the north and enter the opened door.

The Blue Sword Soldier and the two Blue Archers in this dark room must be defeated. One of the Blue Arches hold the small key needed to open the door to the north. Use the torches in the center of the room for light. Once the small key has been obtained, enter the door to the north.

To open the locked door to the right, the two Spear Knights and two Chasupas must be defeated. Once the door opens, travel through it.

In the next room, defeat the two Spear Soldiers to unlock the door to the south.

Two Chasupas and Two Spear Knights are found in this room. The Spear Knight in the center of the room has a small key to unlock the door to the right. It is easiest to defeat all of the enemies in the room. Once the small key has been obtained, enter the locked door.

The next room contains a Sword Knight, a Spear Knight, and a Gold Ball and Chain Trooper. Avoid or defeat them and travel through the door to the north.

In this next room with a doorway in the top-right corner, push the statue to the left to enter the room. Avoid or defeat the Spear Soldier and two Blue Archers. Continue left.

Walk north, across the narrow pathway. Be cautious of the two Blue Sword Soldiers, as they can knock Link off of the edge. It is recommended to use ranged weapons and attacks to avoid being knocked off. Enter the doorway to the north.

The next room has no enemies. Travel north to face Agahnim, the evil wizard and boss of Hyrule Castle Tower.

BOSS BATTLE Agahnim

Link interrupts Agahnim, but not before the evil wizard has used Princess Zelda to break the seal of the seven wise men.

Once Agahnim vanishes, slash the middle curtain to the north to open a secret passageway to the Boss Room.

Agahnim cannot be damaged with regular weapons or the Master Sword. Instead, Link will need to reflect the wizard's attacks back at him. He has three primary attacks:

1. Energy orbs. Use the Master Sword like a baseball bat to send the energy orbs back at Agahnim.
2. Energy ring. Agahnim will shoot six smaller energy orbs in a ring shape. If the energy ring is slashed, it will break apart and shoot in several directions. These smaller energy orbs will not hurt Agahnim if they are reflected back. It is best to avoid this attack.
3. Lightning attack. Agahnim will occasionally stand at the north end of the room. When he does this, he could use one of the first two attack or a lightning attack. The lightning attack will shoot an unblockable stream of lightning directly south. When Agahnim moves to the north end of the room, it is best to stand to the right or left side of him to avoid the lightning.

Link will have to redirect six energy orbs back at Agahnim to defeat him. Once he has been defeated, Agahnim will vanish, teleporting Link into the Dark World.

Palace of Darkness

Total Life   9

Heart Pieces   11.75/24

Having chased Agahnim into the Dark World, Link need to rescue the first of the seven maidens. She is trapped inside of the Palace of Darkness. To enter the palace, he will have to enlist the help of a monkey named Kiki. Once inside, Link must find the Magic Hammer and defeat the Helmasaur King.

As soon as Link is teleported into the Dark World by Agahnim, Sahasrahla will telepathically communicate with Link. He explains that Link must win back the Golden Power and rescue seven maidens from seven dungeons. These seven maidens are descendants of the seven wise men who originally placed the seal. The first maiden is held in the Palace of Darkness.

Quake Medallion

Climb down the Pyramid of Power, traveling right. On the far right side of the pyramid, take a narrow path north to find a Piece of Heart.

Jump off of the pyramid and travel right. The Dark World appears very similar to the light world. Colors are different and so are enemies. Travel to where the Magic Potion Shop would be in the Light World. Here, it is a regular shop. Move the large boulder to the right of the shop and travel north towards the entrance to where Zora's Waterfall would be in the Light World. This is the beginning of the Lake of Ill Omen.

A sign nearby says, "Curses to anyone who throws something into my circle of stones."

Pick up a nearby skull and throw it into the circle of stones to the left of the sign.

A Catfish will appear and give Link the Quake Medallion. The Quake Medallion allows Link to use a jump attack to shake the ground. The entire screen will rumble, causing damage to any enemies in the area.

Entering the Palace of Darkness

Return to the shop. Travel south, along the cliff wall until reaching five statue columns. Travel north, to where the Desert Palace Compound would be in the Light World. On the way, make sure to have least one hundred and ten rupees.

Follow the dirt path to the right until squares in the earth form a triangle pointing northwards. Walk into the opening in the trees at the tip of the arrow. Walk north towards the end of another dirt arrow to exit the trees.

Travel north and all the way to the right. Ignore the pathway in the trees to the north. Continue through an opening to the left.

Travel north and enter the opening in the trees to the right.

In the large area of trees, enter the trees from the north. Look closely at the tree pattern for the small dots. This is the pathway beneath the tree canopy where Link can walk.

Follow it and Link will exit the treeline to the right, followed by a monkey named Kiki. He will ask for ten rupees. Give them to the monkey and he will continue to follow Link. If at any point Kiki leaves, return to this patch of trees and he will reappear. Each time, he will ask for ten rupees.

Walk right and to the north, to the location the entrance to Desert Palace would be in the Light World. Upon arriving, the palace will be locked. Kiki will offer to open it for one hundred rupees. Pay him to open the Palace of Darkness and enter.

The Palace of Darkness

Upon entering the main room of the Palace of darkness, travel towards the closed door on the left. Link will step on a floor tile switch, opening the door. Enter the now opened door.

Defeat or avoid the Helmasaur and enter the door to the north.

Avoid the Medusas in the center of the room. Lift up the pot to the south to reveal a switch. Step on the switch and a treasure chest containing a small key will appear. After collecting the key, return upstairs.

In the room with the Helmasaur, a switch is hidden under the pot to the left on the north side of the room. Step on it to open the door to the south and exit to the main room of the Palace of Darkness.

Palace of Darkness Dungeon Map (Optional)

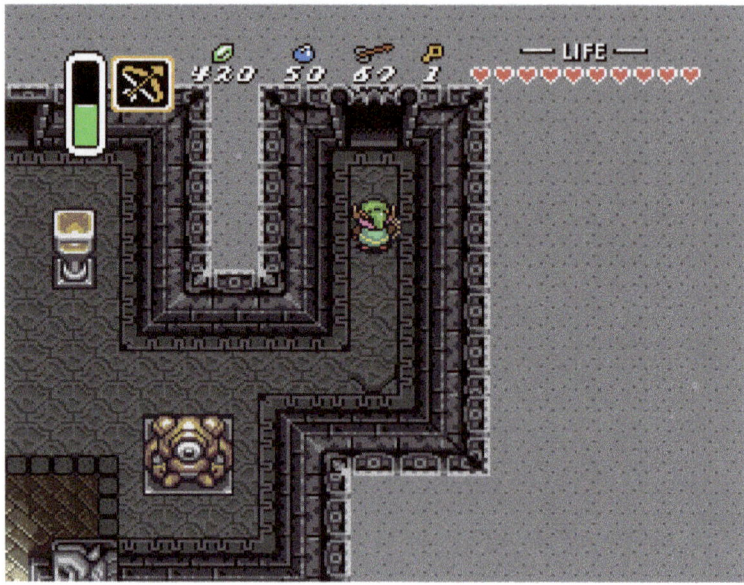

From the main room of the Palace of Darkness, enter the door to the far right. Link may have to step on the switch in the narrow hallway near the door a second time.

Defeat or avoid the Helmasaur in this room and travel down the stairs to the north.

Avoid the Anti-Fairy in this room and step onto the active portal.

To the south of this room is a crack in the wall. Use a Bomb or a dash attack to open the wall and enter.

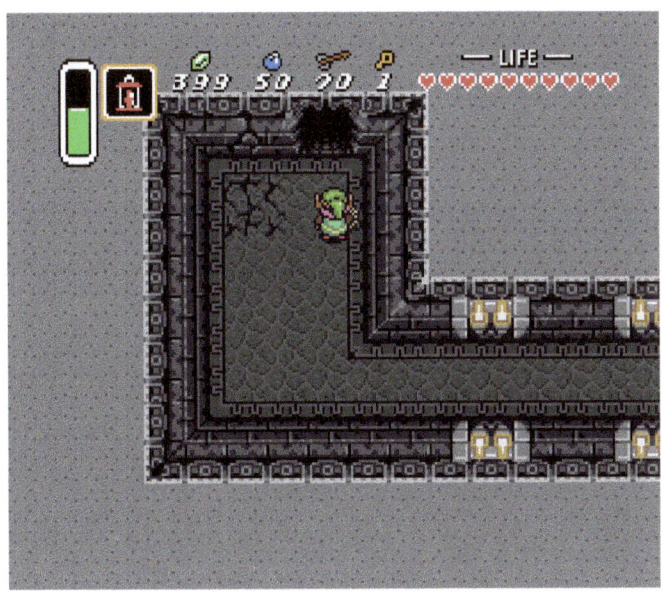

It's easiest to defeat the three Blue Baris while traveling left. To the north of the end of the room is a crack in the wall. Break through it.

In the next room, defeat the Red Goriya and the two Green Goriyas. They mirror Links movements. The Green Goriyas are easy to defeat with sword slashes. The Red Goriya will shoot a fireball if it faces directly towards Link. Stand facing slightly to the right or left or the Red Goriya. Shoot an arrow, then move so that the Red Goriya moves into the path of the arrow. Once the enemies have been defeated, the door to the north will open.

Travel to the door on the north end of the room. The floor will move, pushing Link north or south. Blade Traps move left and right. A Red Bari and two Blue Baris patrol the room. Avoid or defeat the Baris and avoid the Blade Traps to reach the northern end. Enter the door.

Avoid or defeat the three Red Baris and open the treasure chest to obtain the Dungeon Map.

On the right and left sides of the room are cracks in the walls. Open the one to the right to find a Faerie Spring. Open the crack to the left to find a treasure chest containing a small key.

Backtrack towards the main room of the Palace of Darkness. In the room with the four blocks surrounding the portal, move the southern block to the right or left. Step on the portal. Travel through the door to the north.

In the room with the Helmasaur, lift to the right on the northern side of the room to reveal a switch. Step on the switch and exit through the door to the south. Link will now be in the main room of the Palace of Darkness.

The Palace of Darkness Compass

Travel north through the center of the main room of the Palace of Darkness. The next room contains no enemies. Use the small key to open the locked door to the north and enter through it.

Terrorpins and Blue Bari guard this room. The Terrorpins cannot be defeated at this point, so they are best to avoid. On the right side of the room, cross midway across the bridge. Push the block on the right so that falls off of the bridge. Jump off of the bridge, where the block fell.

Link will land on the floor below. Lift the closest skull to reveal a switch. Step on the switch and open the treasure chest that appears to collect another small key. Be careful as four Yellow Stalfos will drop from the ceiling. Lift a skull in the right corner and step on the portal.

Travel through the door to the north.

Move the statue on the left to the left. Enter the door to the north.

Back in the room with the Blue Baris and Terrorpins, travel left. In the middle of this bridge, place a bomb on the cracked part of the floor. Fall through the hole.

Walk north and open the locked door by using a small key.

Open the treasure chest to collect the Big Key. Jump off of the ledge to the right to fall one floor down.

Take the portal again, then travel through the doorway to the north. Once again, push the statue to the left and enter the door to the north. Travel right, back to the bridge with the blocks. This time, cross the bridge and enter the doorway.

Unlock the treasure chest to obtain a small key. Stand on the arrow sign and move to the north to jump the gap.

Walk to the left, down the narrow path and open the locked door by using a small key.

This room is can be very challenging. Past the pots, the floor will quickly crumble. There are also two Helmasaurs on the path. The best strategy is to pick up one skull and quickly run across the path, defeating the first Helmasaur by throwing the skull. Defeat the second Helmasaur with a beam from the sword if Link has full health. If not, use a dash attack, the Ether Medallion, the Quake Medallion, or Magic Powder. Once it has been defeated, quickly lift up the skull and enter the door to the right.

Open the treasure chest guarded by four Terrorpins to collect the Dungeon Compass. Walk down either of the staircases to the north.

The Magic Hammer

Light the torch next to the door, then collect the blue rupees by heading south.

At the end of the room, open both treasure chests (one contains arrows and one contains a small key). Collect the blue rupees on the opposite side of the room and exit through the nearest door.

Do not use the small key on the door to the south as it is a simply a way back to a previous room and a waste of a key. Instead, walk through the door to the left.

Open the door on the left using a small key.

This room is a dark maze, filled with Green Kodongos. In the north corner to the left is a treasure chest filled with Bombs. From that treasure chest, travel south, then east to another treasure chest containing a small key.

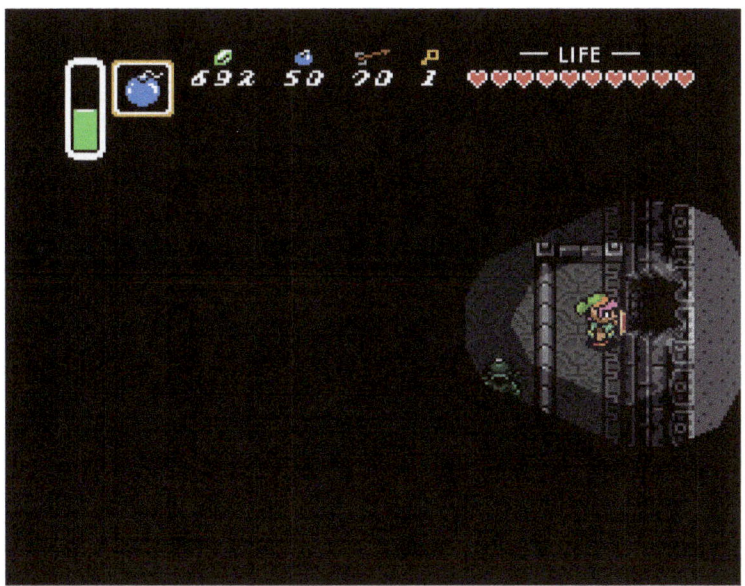

Travel north and to the right from the small key. There is a crack in the wall. Use a Bomb to open a hole in the wall and enter.

Collect the Magic Hammer from the large treasure chest. The Magic Hammer is useful against many enemies. Hitting the ground with the Magic Hammer will flip many enemies upside down. It can also whack mole heads and flatten stakes.

Finding the Palace of Darkness Boss Room

Backtrack through the dark maze room. In the room with the disintegrating floor, quickly walk across the falling hallway. Exit through the door to the south.

Follow the path right. Midway across, use the arrow to jump onto the platform to the south.

Defeat the Hardhat Beetles and use a ranged attack to hit the crystal. The crystal switch should turn blue and the blue blocks to the right will lower. Pass the lowered blue blocks and head through the door to the right

On the north side of the room is a locked door. Lift the three skulls to the right to reveal a floor switch. Push the closest statue onto the switch to keep the door open. Enter the door to the north.

Defeat the mirrored Red Goriya and the two mirrored Green Gorias, then walk through the door to the north.

A Blade Trap moves right and left across the room. Carefully pass it and hit the crystal switch to turn it red. The red blocks to the left will lower.

Travel right to the statue. Use an arrow to shoot it in the eye. The right will will move, revealing a staircase. Take the staircase down.

The next two rooms will be dark, without any torches. Use the Magic Hammer to whack the mole heads. Walk behind the line of lowered red blocks, then use a ranged weapon to hit the red crystal switch to the right. The red block will rise and the blue blocks will lower. Exit through the door to the locked door to the left by using a small key.

Walk down the narrow hallway, defeating the Terrorpin and exiting through the door to the south.

This room has two torches near the center of the room that can be lit by using the lamp. There are also six Terrorpins. Be careful when using the Magic Hammer. Knocking the ground with the Magic Hammer will flip the Terrorpins on their backs. Knocking the ground a second time will flip the Terrorpins back on their feet. Defeat all of them to open the door to the left.

There are two torches in this room that can be lit and no enemies. Push the right block on the north side to the south. Step on the portal.

Walk north and defeat the four Terrorpins. The door to the north contains the boss of the Palace of Darkness.

Boss Room The Helmasaur King

Along with dealing damage whenever it touches Link, the Helmasaur King has a variety of attack to guard the Palace of Darkness. Avoid all of the Helmasaur King's attacks as much as possible.

Its long tail constantly swings. Occasionally, it will speed up this swinging and stretch the tail further, creating a larger path of danger. Stand directly in front of the boss to avoid the tail.

The Helmasaur King can also shoot fireballs. It will shoot a single fireball. This fireball with transform into three. Those three will then turn into four. This means there are a total of twelve possible fireballs for each original fireball. These fireballs will always split diagonally, so try to stay perpendicular.

Because the Helmasaur King hides its weak spot beneath its helmet, Link must first remove the helmet using Bombs or the Magic Hammer. Using Bombs is recommended as it will only take three direct Bombs to remove the helmet. The Magic Hammer will take several more hits.

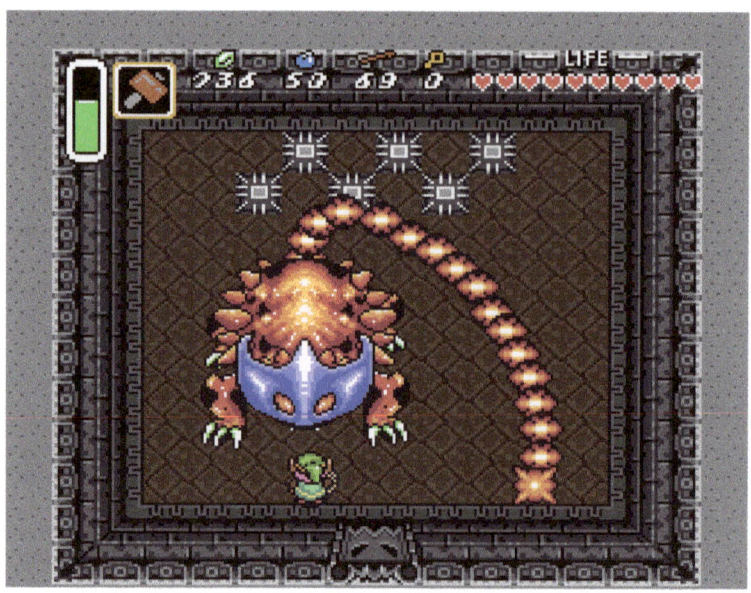

After the helmet has broken off, the green jewel on the top of its head will be vulnerable. Use Arrows or the Master Sword. Hit the green jewel seven times to defeat the Helmasaur King.

Once the Helmasaur King has been defeated, collect the Piece of Heart and then the first Crystal. This first Crystal contains the first of the seven maidens. She explains that all seven maidens are need to open a larger gate between the Light and Dark Worlds. The next maiden is in Swamp Palace.

Swamp Palace

Total Life 11

Heart Pieces 12/24

The next dungeon that Link must face is Swamp Palace, located over the Swamp Ruins in the Dark World. Before heading into Swap Palace, Link must collect the Flute. The Bomba Medallion and Cane of Bryna are also available, though they are not required to complete the game. Once in Swamp Palace, Link must face the dungeon boss and rescue the second maiden.

Extra Items (Optional)

Before entering Swamp Palace, there are several extra items for Link to collect. None of these are required for the main quest line, but some may offer support (Pieces of Heart, rupees, etc.).

From the Palace of Darkness, travel left and south. Near the five statue columns to the south, use the Magic Hammer to whack a path through the stakes. Continue south.

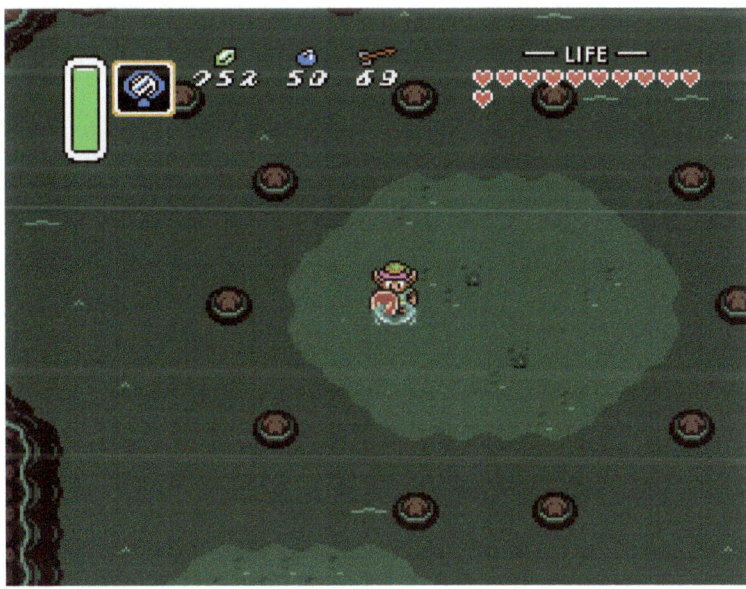

Jump into the water and stand inside the lighter circle area. Use the Magic Mirror to teleport back to the Light World.

Avoid the Buzz Blob and collect the Piece of Heart.

If Link does not have a fully upgraded Bomb and Arrow holding capacity from the Pond of Happiness, now is a good time to trade in those rupees. Travel south and to the right to locate the island containing the cave to the Pond of Happiness.

Travel left and to the north to exit lake Hylia just north of the where Link collected the Piece of Heart. Continue north to where the bridge starts. Walk left, then to an opening in the cliffs to the south. Follow the cliff wall left, slashing through a group of bushes. Use the Magic hammer to whack a path through the stakes. Lift up the boulder to the north and step on the portal to the Dark World.

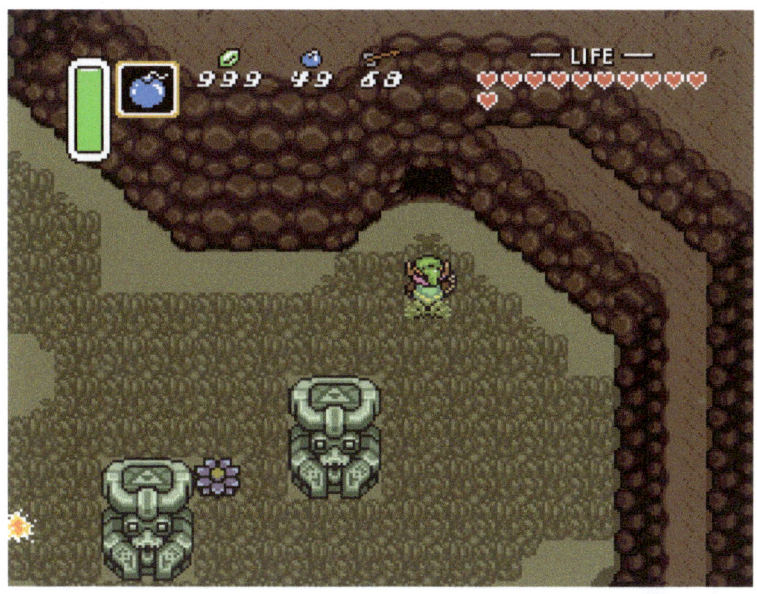

Use the Magic Hammer on the stakes to the right and continue right. Slash through the bushes. Continue right to find a crack in the cliff wall to the north. Open the hole and enter.

Inside, speak with the person to earn three hundred rupees. Use a bomb on the crack in the north wall to receive an additional eighty rupees in four treasure chests.

Exit the cave and travel north. Follow the cliff wall to the left and then south until reaching a diamond shape made with flowers. Stand inside of or next to the diamond and use the Magic Mirror to teleport back to the Light World.

Walk inside the nearby cave. Break the pots and collect the Piece of Heart.

Back outside, step into the warp portal created by the Magic Mirror to re-enter the Dark World. Travel north.

The Flute

Travel to the arrow made of flowers, located just left of the southern central section of the Dark World.

Slash the flowers to travel north.

On a stump sits Flute Boy. Talk to him to receive the Shovel. This Shovel will allow Link to dig up the Flute.

Walk slightly south of Flute Boy and use the Magic mirror to teleport to the Light World. Do not teleport too close to Dark World Flute Boy as Light World Flute Boy will automatically freeze Link when he warps into the Light World.

Just to the north and left of Light World Flute Boy is a group of moving flowers and grass. Use the Shovel in the center to dig up the Flute.

Use the Magic Mirror's portal to return to Dark World and speak with Dark World Flute Boy again. Flute Boy will give Link the Flute, but asks that Link plays the Flute one last time. After Link plays, Flute Boy will turn into a stump.

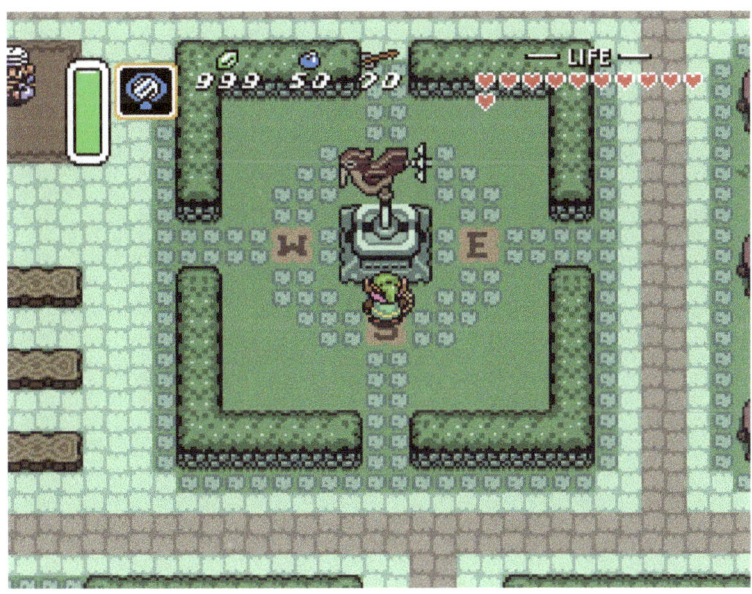

Return to the Light World by using the Magic Mirror and travel to Kakariko Village. In the center of the village is a Weathercock. Stand to the south of it and play the Flute.

The Weathercock will transform into a duck. Now, whenever Link plays the Flute, the duck will fly Link to one of several locations. This allows for much speedier travel.

Extra Items 2 (Optional)

Exit Kakariko through the road to the right. A house sits on top of a ledge, cuccos wander around, and there is a cave just south of the house. Beside the cave is an opening in the ground. Link can jump into this from above. Whack the stake blocking the path above the hole and jump down.

Once inside the cave, walk through the door to the north.

Use Magic Powder on the red goblet and Batter will appear. He's grumpy from being awoken and will 'curse' Link. Really, Batter reduces the amount of magic that magic items and attacks consume by half. Exit the cave and return to Kakariko Village.

Travel to the left and north to a narrow path leading into the Lost Woods. Avoid or defeat the three Blue Sword Soldiers and enter the woods.

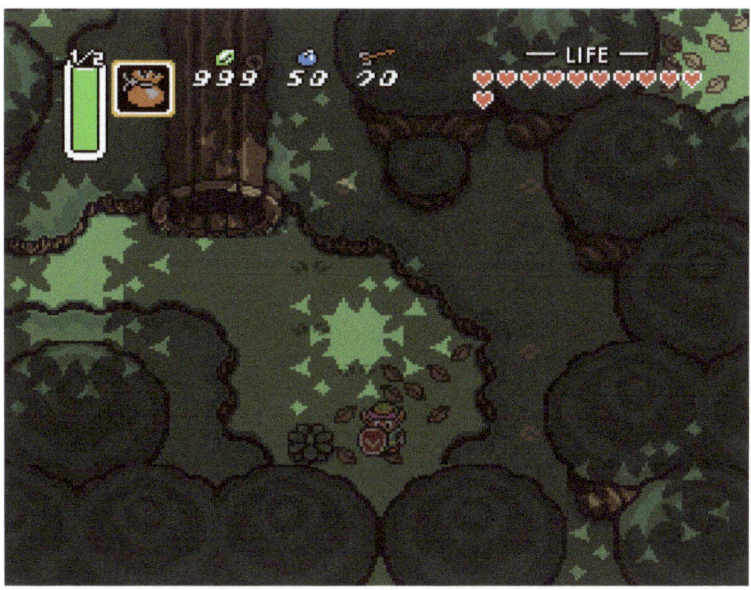

Take the path immediately to the right. At the end of the trail, walk between the two trees to the south to exit the Lost Woods.

Walk south and use the Magic Hammer to whack the stakes. Lift the nearby boulder and step on the now exposed portal to the Dark World.

Follow the path to the left, slashing through the long line of bushes.

Head south to the Village of Outcasts. In the nearest house to the south is the Treasure Chest Game.

Speak to the shop owner to start the game. It costs thirty rupees for Link to open two treasure chests. While Link can win Arrows, Bombs, hearts, and rupees, the real prize is a Piece of Heart. The locations are completely randomized. Keep playing until Link receives the Piece of Heart.

Travel to the right, to the house located on the opposite side of the square from the Treasure Chest Game. Inside, the home is an odd 'C' shape. Collect three hundred rupees from inside the treasure chest and exit the house.

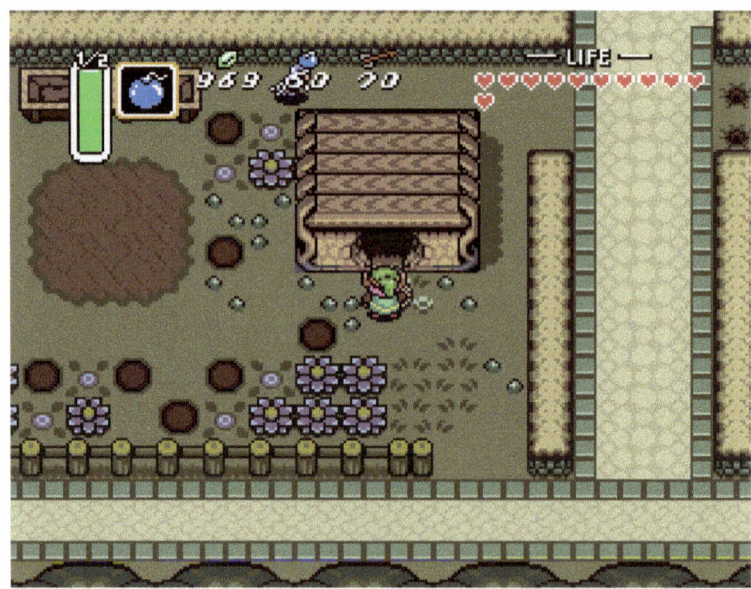

Next, travel to where the shop with the Cuccos was located in Kakariko Village. The hut has a crack along its southern wall. Use a Bomb to open an entry and go inside to collect 300 rupees from a treasure chest.

Exit the Village of Outcasts through the northern gate and travel right to where the Hyrulian Cemetery would be in the Light World. This is the Ghostly Garden. The gravestone that Link moved in the Light World is, instead, a pile of five boulders. Use a dash attack to clear the boulder from the path. Travel right and up the stairs.

Once on the ledge, use the Magic Mirror to teleport to the Light World. Enter the cave and break the pots.

Use a Bomb on the northern wall to create an entryway. Walk inside and collect a Piece of Heart. Exit the cave and use the Magic Mirror's portal to return to the Dark World.

Walk to the right of the steps, slash the bush, and discover another pile of five boulders. Stand near the pile and use the Magic Mirror to go to the Dark World.

Stand to the south of the gravestone and use the dash attack to move the gravestone northward. Fall into the hole.

Open the treasure chest to receive the Magic Cape. This allows Link to become invisible. While he is invisible, Link will not take damage. The Magic Cape drains the Magic Meter quickly, so use it wisely.

Exit the grave and use the Magic Mirror's portal to return to the Dark World. Travel to where the Twin Lumberjack's house would be in the Light World.

Use the Magic Mirror to teleport to the Light World. The Twin Lumberjacks are no longer around, but the tree that they were sawing is still standing (though, it is now discolored). Use the dash attack to to make the tree collapse inwards. Fall into the hole.

Inside, there is a Faerie Spring to the north, Travel through the door to the right to collect a Piece of Heart. Exit the cave by jumping into the pool to the right and walking south. Return to the Magic Mirror's portal and travel to the Dark World.

Journey back to the to the Village of Outcasts. Head through the southern gate and keep to the right while jumping down the cliffs.

Once at the bottom, travel left to find the Digging Game Operator. For eighty rupees, Link can play the Digging Game. Link has thirty seconds to dig up as many things as possible. Most of these will be rupees or Magic Potions. The real prize is a Piece of Heart. The Digging Game is randomized and relies mostly on luck. For this reason, the Digging Game can be the most tedious portion of *A Link to the Past*.

An unofficial theory to increase chances has been discussed among players. It is speculated that Link must dig twenty five holes before there is even a chance for the Piece of Heart to appear. For european releases, this number is as low as twenty.

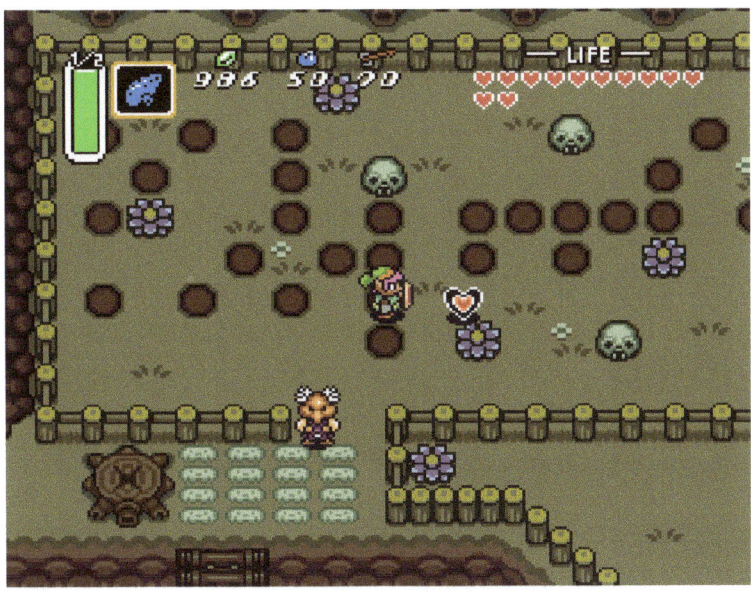

Whether these ideas are true or not, the more holes Link digs, the better his chances of finding the Piece of Heart. Be persistent. Exit the screen by traveling right to reset the game before retrying.

Bomba Medallion (Optional)

Once Link has collected the Piece of Heart from the Digging game, exit the Village of Outcasts by following the path to the right. Continue following the path until reaching the large boulder to the south. Lift the boulder and walk south, keeping left along the cliff. Follow the narrow trail to the left, between two cliffs.

Near where the transition of grass to desert would be on the lower left side of the Light World is a triangle of flowers and grass. Sand in or near it and use the Magic Mirror to teleport to the Light World.

In the Light World, Link is on top of a raised cliff. Walk to the left and read the tablet using the Book of Mudora.

Link will raise the Master Sword and gain the final medallion, the Bombos Medallion. Although this medallion is not required to complete the game, it is the most powerful. When used, the Bombos Medallion defeats all enemies on the screen.

Cane of Byrna (Optional)

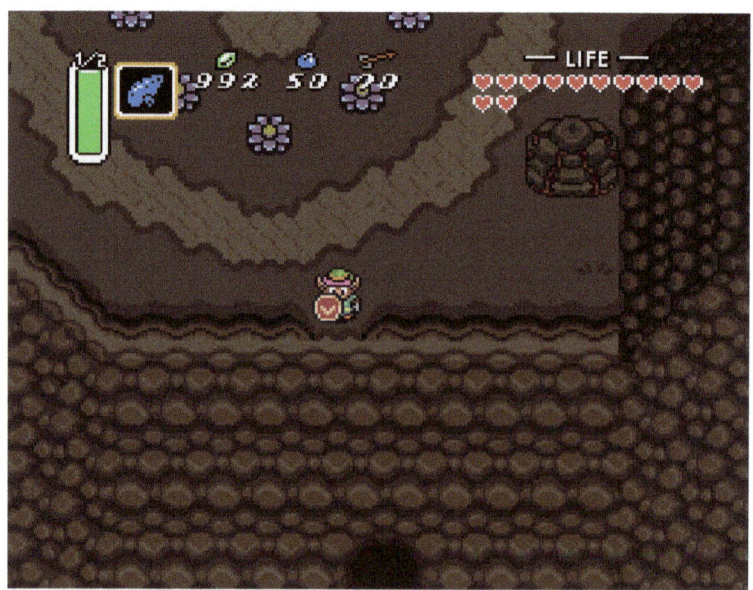

Use the Flute to travel to Location #1, Death Mountain. Scale the mountain all the way to the warp point at the top. Make sure to have bottled fairies or lots of health. Step onto the warp portal to enter the Dark World. Walk directly south and jump onto the ledge below. Enter the cave.

Whack the mole heads with the Magic Hammer, then use the Magic Cape to run across the spikes. Follow the path, using a dash attack as much as possible to move quickly. The Magic Cap will quickly deplete Link's Magic Meter.

At the end of the cave, lift the larger boulder out of the way and open the treasure chest to receive the Cane of Byrna. This item surrounds Link in a bright light, not only protecting him from enemies, but dealing damage to any enemies that come into contact with it. Like the Magic Cape, the Cane of Byrna requires magic to use. Unlike the Magic Cape, the Cane of Byrna will not allow Link to move through enemies.

Link's Magic Meter will now most likely be empty. Drink a Green Potion or prepare a bottled fairy. The eight skulls in the room all contain hearts. Dash back to the entrance of the cave, moving quickly to lessen the damage the spikes cause. Once outside, use the Magic Mirror to teleport back to the Light Word.

Entering Swamp Palace

Use the Flute to travel to Location #4, Link's house. Walk south to the Great Swamp, then to the left. Follow the cliff wall to reach the stakes blocking the Dark World Portal. Whack the stakes, lift the boulder, and enter the Dark World.

Travel south to where the Great Ruins would be in the Light World. Use the Magic Mirror to teleport back to the Light World. Enter the ruins.

Move the middle block up and one of the other blocks to the side to enter the room to the north. Pull one of the levers, opening the floodgates. Exit the Swamp Ruins.

Use the Magic Mirror portal to travel to the Dark World. With the floodgates opened, Link can now enter what would be the Swamp Ruins in the Light World. This is Swamp Palace in the Dark World.

Swamp Palace Dungeon Map

Enter the water and swim to the left. Climb the short stairwell. A Blade Trap moves right and left. Three Hovers glide on the water. To the north is a Water Gibo.

Defeat the Hovers for a treasure chest to appear. Collect the small key from the treasure chest and enter the locked door to the north.

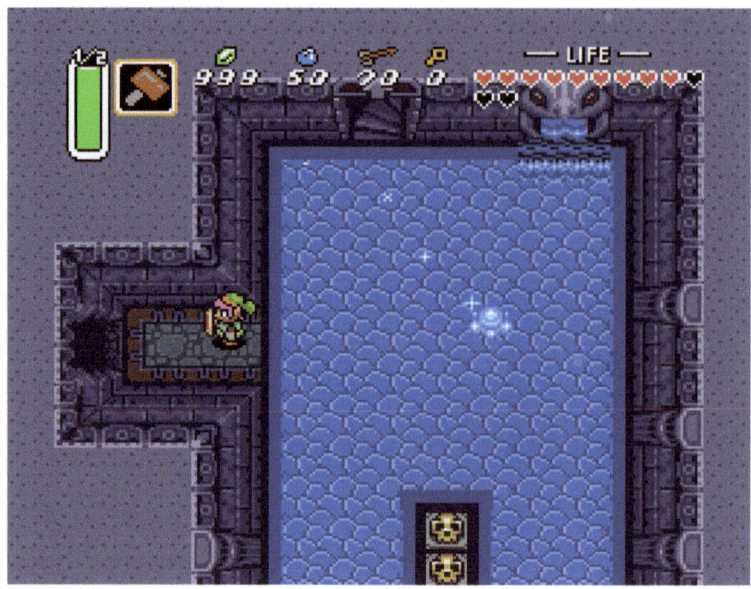

To the left, in a narrow section, is a cracked wall. Use a Bomb to open the wall and enter.

Avoid or defeat the Red Zols and open the treasure chest to receive the Dungeon Map.

Return to the previous room. Avoid or defeat the enemies in the room. The most southern skull hides a small key. Lift up the skull to retrieve it. Exit through the locked door to the south and left.

Avoid or defeat the various enemies and travel south, down the stairs. Walk through the opened door to the north.

Lift the skull to obtain another small key, then exit to the south.

Walk up the stairs and through the locked door to the left.

Defeat the Red and Blue Stalfos. Use the Magic Hammer to whack the mole heads. Next, push the lever for the right to the left. Water should begin to flood the lower level of the dungeon.

The wall to the left has a crack that can be opened. Once the entryway has been made, enter to find two pots containing a blue rupee and a Bomb. Return to the previous room and exit through the door to the south.

Jump into the water and swim up the stairs to the left. Enter the opened door on the left wall to enter the main room of Swamp Palace.

Swamp Palace Compass (Optional)

Travel down the stairs and go through the southern door.

Follow the path right, through another opened door.

Continue down the path and through the door.

Push the southern block to the right. A treasure chest containing the Dungeon Compass will appear to the left. Collect the compass and head through the door to the north, back to the main room of Swamp Palace.

The Hookshot

Climb up the steps on the left side and enter the opened door.

Avoid or defeat the enemies in this room. Walk down the step to the left and enter the open door to the north.

Lift the skull to collect another small key before exiting the room to the south.

Climb back up the stairs, through the room filled with various enemies and traps, and back to the main room of Swamp Palace. Use the stairs to get back into the water. Travel north, up another set of stairs to the left, and open the locked door.

Avoid or defeat the enemies in the room. Use the Master Sword to slash the crystal switch in the room and the blue blocks should go down. Push the lever, causing more water to flow. Strike the crystal switch again, causing the blue blocks to rise, then exit the room through the door to the right.

Travel back into the water in the main room of Swamp Palace and back through the door to the south and left. This time, Link can swim over the blocks and up the stairs to the left. Travel through the open door.

Avoid the enemies and traps. Walk down the stairs to the left and towards the blocks. Push the southern block to the left and the middle block to the north. Travel up the stairs and through the doorway to the north.

Push the block to the right. Travel north and to the right. Push the block northward and fall down the hole.

The red blocks should be lowered. Travel through the door to the right.

Open the treasure chest to receive the Big Key. Exit back through the door to the right. Jump off the ledge.

Optionally, Link can move the blocks to the left and travel back to the room with the holes. Push the northern block on the left side of the room up and fall down the hole. Collect the red rupee from the treasure chest, then jump down into the water.

Backtrack to the main room of Swamp Palace. Climb up the stairs in the center of the room and open the large treasure chest. Link will receive the Hookshot. This item stretches across the length of the screen. It can stun and/or damage enemies, pull items towards Link, or pull Link towards items. It can latch onto pots, skulls, and treasure chests.

Finding Swamp Palace Boss Room

Use the Hookshot to latch onto the skull to the right. This will pull Link over to the platform. Lift the skull on the far right to find a small key.

Jump back into the water and climb back onto the platform with the now opened large treasure chest. Use the Hookshot to pull Link towards the skulls to the north. Open the locked door and enter.

Travel to the left and defeat the Red Bari. Next, lift the pot in the north corner to find a switch. Move the statue onto the switch to open the nearest door as well as one on the right side of the room.

Walk to the right side of the room and enter the newly opened door to the left.

Avoid or defeat the Red Bari and head through the door to the north.

Push the lever to the left, causing the water to lower. Walk down the stairs and through the left door.

Optionally, follow the narrow passageway south and through an open door. Open the treasure chests for two red rupees, then travel back through the door to the left and up the narrow passageway.

Travel through the door to the north.

Optionally, the open door on the far left side of this room can be entered for six skulls containing rupees, Bombs, and Arrows.

In the room with the six blocks, the third block from the left can be pushed to the right to reveal a treasure chest containing one red rupee.

There are six mouths with flowing water along the northern wall. The second from the right contains a hidden doorway beneath it. Travel through it.

Head up the stairs and through the door to the north.

Walk south, through an open door.

In the next room, jump into the water and climb the stairs to the right. Underneath the skull is a small key to be collected.

Optionally, swim to the stairs in the middle of the room. Use a Bomb on the cracked way to open an entryway. There are a series of eight skulls here containing Bombs, Arrows, Magic Jars, and hearts. Return through the door to the south.

Swim to the door on the left side of the room and open it.

Follow the hallway north to the entrance of the Boss Room.

BOSS BATTLE Arrghus

Arrhgus is a giant one-eyed jellyfish-like boss. It is surrounded by smaller enemies known as Arrgi. Before Link can battle Arrhgus, every single Arrgi must be defeated.

To defeat the Arrgi, use the Hookshot to pull a single Arrgi away from the mass of enemies. Two slashes from the Master Sword will defeat the Arrgi.

Occasionally, the Arrgi will form a spinning ring around Arrghus to increase their attack area. Avoid touching any enemies. Repeat this Hookshot process until all of the Arrgi have been defeated.

Once Arrghus is no longer protected by the Arrgi, it will begin to slam itself into the water. This is followed by it quickly bouncing off of the walls. Avoid being touched and slash it with the Master Sword (eight hits required) or hit it with the Ice Rod (four hits). If Link uses the Master Sword, a spin attack will be the easiest to hit Arrghus with as it covers more area.

Once Arrghus has been defeated, collect the Piece of Heart and the second Crystal. The second maiden will tell Link about the Triforce that was hidden in the Golden Land as well as some lore about Ganon.

Skull Woods

Total Life   13

Heart Pieces   18.5/24

The third maiden is imprisoned in Skull Woods. To rescue her, Link will have to explore the area, dropping into holes and secret passageways to enter different sections of the dungeon. After collecting the Fire Rod, Link will be prepared to face the Skull Woods boss and free the maiden.

Death Mountain Piece of Heart (Optional)

Use the Magic Mirror to travel back to the Light world. Once there, use the Flute to go to Location #3, Kakariko Village. Travel north and to the left to enter the Lost woods.

Take the path to the left and south through the opening between the two large trees.

Whack the stake and lift the boulder to teleport to the Dark World.

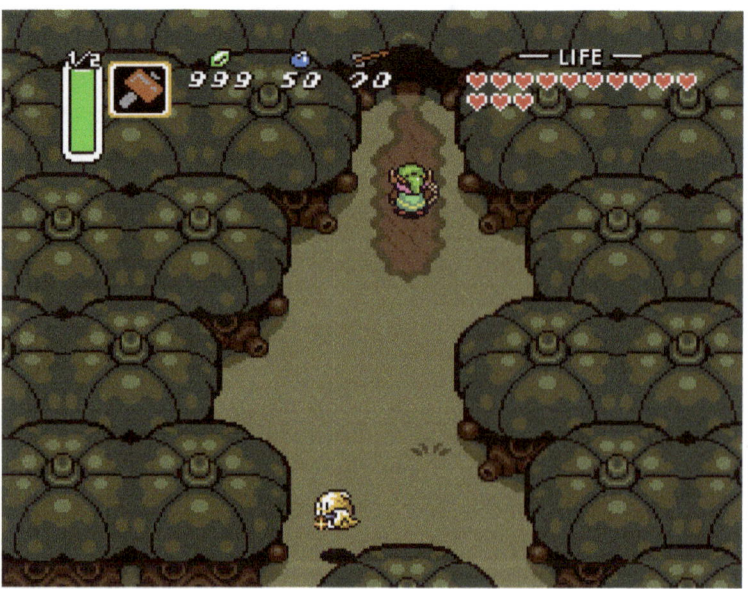

Travel north, into The Skeleton Forest.

Follow the path to the right, lifting skulls and slashing flowers to clear the path. Exit the woods to the south.

Go to the right and north to find where the entrance to Death mountain would be if Link were in the Light World. Lift the Boulder and enter the cave.

Follow the passage north, avoiding or defeating enemies, and enter the open doorway.

Use the Hookshot to cross the hole to the south by aiming at the skulls.

Activate the Magic Cape to walk through the Bumper and exit the cave through the southern door.

Collect the Piece of Heart and drop down from the cliff.

Entering Skull Woods

Skull Woods is different from the other dungeons in two aspects. First, it uses the overworld as transitions between dungeon rooms. Second, a large majority of these dungeon rooms are not necessary. For that reason, this guide will focus on the most efficient path.

Located where the Lost Woods would be in the Light World, Skeleton Forest has several entrances. Enter the woods through the entrance just north of the northern gate of the Village of Outcasts.

Walk north and to the left to find a hole in the ground. This hole leads to the Dungeon Map. To skip this area, stay to the south, lift the flower, and continue north.

Skull Woods Dungeon Map and Compass (Optional)

To obtain the Dungeon Map and Compass, travel south and to the left. Take the first path north and fall into the hole.

Walk south through the room, avoiding or defeating the enemies. Be careful not to fall off of the edge. Travel through the door to the right.

On the north side of the room, open the treasure chest to receive the Dungeon Compass. Holes will open in the floor. Exit through the door to the south and to the right.

Be careful of the Wallmaster and avoid or defeat the enemies in the room. Lift the three skull in front of the treasure chest to open it. Inside is a small key. Exit through the door to the north.

Use the Hookshot to reach the Treasure Chest and Obtain the Dungeon Map. Exit the room by carefully walking diagonally between the holes in the floor and traveling through the door to the left.

Exit back to the Skeleton Forest through the door to the south.

The Fire Rod

Travel north to the parallel ribcage pathways. Travel north, then follow the path south.

Enter the dungeon through the skull mouth.

Defeat all of the enemies in the room and be cautious of the Wallmaster. The easiest way to do this is to use the Bombos Medallion. Lift the skull in the center of the room, then drag the right statue onto the switch. Enter the newly opened door to the north.

Again, defeat the enemies and be cautious of the Wallmaster. Collect the Big Key from the treasure chest. A Bomb can be used to open the cracked wall to the right. Inside is a skull containing a Magic Potion.

Backtrack out of this part of the dungeon and back to Skeleton Forest. Follow the ribcage path to the north, then back south. In the center of the nine flowers is a hole. Drop down into it.

It is easiest to defeat the Helmasaur by throwing a skull at it. Avoid or defeat the Hardhat Beetle. Use a Bomb on the cracked left wall to open it. Travel through the new opening.

Carefully walk around the edges of the holes to reach the lever in the center of the room. Pull it and the southern wall will explode, opening a new area.

Defeat the two Mini-Moldorms before opening the large treasure chest to receive the Fire Rod. This item shoots fireballs at enemies, doing damage. It can also be used to light torches from a distance.

Use the Hookshot on one of the statues to pull Link across the holes in the floor. Exit through the door to the south.

Finding Skull Woods Boss Room

Travel back north, then south through the ribcage tunnels and re-enter the dungeon through the mouth of the skull. Back in the room with the switch and the statue, travel through the door to the left.

Continue left, through another open door.

Collect the key from the left skull, then exit through the door to the south.

Back in the Skeleton Forest, walk north, through the ribcage to the left.

Use the Fire Rod on the giant skull to open a doorway.

Although Link should have one small key, if he does not, follow the path to the left and through a series of rooms to acquire one. If Link does have one key, walk north and open the locked door.

Two Blue Baris, a Red Bari, and a Wallmaster guard this room. Additionally, there are several stars on the floor that change the positioning of the holes. Although Link can carefully walk around the narrow edges of the holes, this is very risky. Instead, step to the stars in the center. Then lift the skulls in the bottom left corner and step on the star. Next, travel to the skulls in the top left corner. Lift the skulls and step on the stars just north and to the right of the center of the room. Step on the star in the top right corner. Lift the skull and exit through the door to the right.

Several Gibdos patrol this room. It is best to defeat them with the Bombos Medallion before traveling. The Fire Rod can also be used. A Wallmaster also drops from the ceiling. In order to open the door on the north side of the room, all four torches must be lit. Three of the four torches can be lit with the lamp, but the final torch on the north end of the room will require the Fire Rod. This must be done quickly, before the torches extinguish. The skulls in this room hold Magic Potions incase Link is running low. Once the door opens, travel through it.

Avoid or defeat the enemies in this room. Slash at the center of the north wall of this room to reveal a hidden doorway. Enter it.

In this room, all of the enemies must be defeated for a small key to appear. It is quickest to use the Bombos Medallion. Once the key drops, travel through the locked door to the right.

The hole in this room leads to the Boss Room. Be sure to collect the Magic Potion from the northern skull pot before dropping down the hole.

BOSS BATTLE Mothula

Skull Woods is defended by Mothula. Blade aTraps also slide across the moving floor. If Link touches Mothula or one of the Blade Traps, he will lose two hearts. Mothula also shoots three streams of fire beams. These also cause two hearts worth of damage.

There are three weapons that Mothula is vulnerable to: the Master Sword, Fire Rod, and the Magic Hammer. The Master sword is the least powerful against Mothula. It will take only eight hits with the Fire Rod or four hits with the Magic Hammer to defeat the boss.

If Link has a Bee, the Bee will attack and distract Mothula, allowing Link to attack more easily. Using the Magic Cape will also help Link by avoiding the Blade Traps, but it will drain magic quickly.

Once Mothula has been defeated, collect the Piece of Heart and the third Crystal. The third maiden will tell Link of the prophecy of the Great Cataclysm. This prophecy outlines the requirements of a hero and what events cause a hero to appear.

Gargoyle's Domain

Total Life   14

Heart Pieces   19.75/24

There are no side quests to complete before entering the fourth dungeon, so Link can journey directly to Gargoyle's Domain. Once inside, he will need to rescue a woman from a cell, collect the Titan's Gloves, and discover a startling surprise after leading the helpless woman to the light. The boss of Gargoyle's Domain is the leader of the Gang of Thieves and Link must defeat him if the fourth maiden is to be rescued.

Finding Gargoyle's Domain

Exit the Skeleton Forest by heading south and into the skull mouth.

Travel left, through two rooms, then exit back into the Skeleton Forest through the door to the south.

Go north through the ribcage, then south. Stay to the south of the hole in the ground and be careful not to fall in. Exit through the two trees to the south.

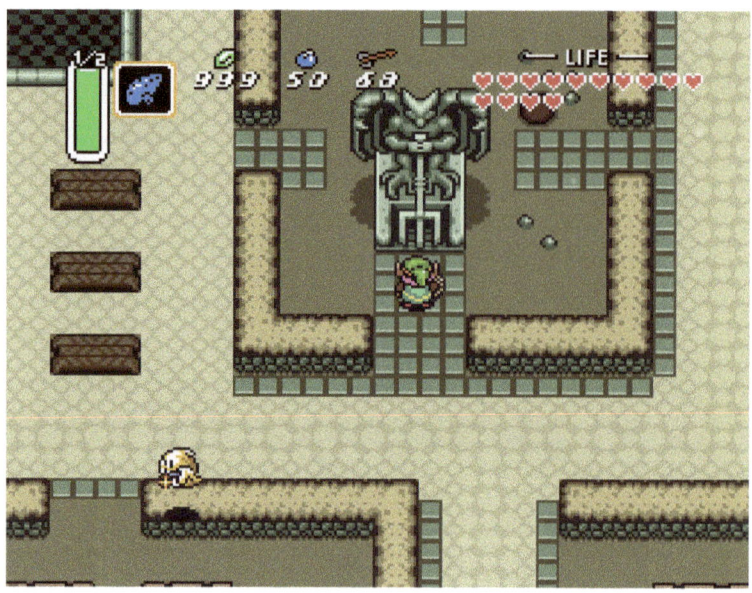

In the center of the Village of Outcasts is a large Gargoyle Statue. Pull the pitchfork that the Gargoyle Statue is holding to open the dungeon entrance.

Gargoyle's Domain Dungeon Map and Compass (Optional)

After entering Gargoyle's Domain, travel north and to the left corner. Jump down to the treasure chest.

Open the treasure chest to receive the Dungeon Map.

Travel all the way to the right and head north.

Continue down the immediate path to the right.

Immediately turn south.

Climb the stairs and continue south. Open the treasure chest to obtain the Dungeon Compass. Jump to the floor below and travel left.

Open another chest to collect the Big Key. Skip the next section of this guide, titled Gargoyle's Domain Big Key.

Gargoyle's Domain Big Key

Walk to the north. In the right corner of the room, jump down to the floor below. Follow the path north, immediately right, and immediately south.

Climb the steps to the south, then jump back down. Travel left to find a treasure chest.

Open the treasure chest and collect the Big Key.

The Titan's Mitt

From the treasure chest containing the Big Key, travel north one screen. Climb the staircase on the right side of the room.

Unlock the door to the north on the right side by using the Big Key.

Avoid or defeat the various Stalfos while walking north. When you reach a pair of pillars by a north-facing door, lift the skull on the right side to find a small key.

Travel to the south side of the room and enter the locked door to the left.

Avoid or defeat the enemies in this room and exit through the door to the left.

Avoid the enemies and continue left.

Travel through the open door to the north, avoiding the enemies.

Lift the skull to find another small key in a room filled with Blade Traps. Stand just north of the blue block on the left side.

Use the Boomerang to hit the crystal switch before exiting the room through the northern door.

Lift the southern skull closest to the right wall. Step on the switch that appears and the right door will open. Enter it.

Walk down the long hallway to reach an open door on the right side of the room.

In the next room, the treasure chest contains Bombs. Open it if Link is running low. Throw one of the Bombs at the crack in the floor. This will allow light to enter the room below.

Return down the long hallway, down the stairs to the room with the Blade Traps, and back to the narrow room with the moving floor. Enter the door to the right that is no longer blocked by a red block.

Avoid or defeat the enemies and travel through the door to the right.

The floor moves in several directions in this room .Move quickly and enter the door to the north.

It may be easier to defeat the enemies in this room before lifting the large block in the center of the room out of the way. After the large block has been removed, travel through the door to the south.

Travel through the door on the right.

Follow the path, defeating the Zazaks along the way, until Link reaches a woman in a cell. Collect the small key out of the nearby treasure chest and then speak with the woman. She thanks Link and asks him to take her outside. From this point on, the woman will follow Link through the dungeon.

Travel south to exit the cell room.

Head through the door to the left, past the well in the middle.

Again, go through the door to the left.

Whack a mole head and open the large treasure chest. Link will receive the Titan's Mitt. This is an upgrade from the Power Glove and allows Link to lift heavier boulders.

Helping the Woman

Quickly exit the room through the door to the right, as the floor has begun to crumble. If the floor has already crumbled, use the Hookshot on one of the statues. Continue traveling right through the next room.

Enter the door to the north.

Lift the large block and go up the stairs to the north.

Now in the room with the floor that moves in several directions, lift the northern skull on the right side of the room. Step on the switch and the right door will open. Enter it.

Prepare for the boss battle before traveling through the north door.

BOSS BATTLE Blind

Walk the woman into the light. She will begin to transform into the Gargoyle's Domain dungeon boss, Blind. Also known as the leader of the Gang of Thieves, Blind sought the Triforce and was transformed into a demon by the Dark World's curse.

Blind begins by shooting laser beams while rotating between hovering either to the north or south. His head is his only vulnerable spot and Link can attack it with the Master Sword. Once Link lands a slash to Blind's head, fireballs will shoot in four diagonal directions.

After three hits to the head, Blind's head will detach itself from the body and begin spinning around the room. The head will also shoot energy beams. Blind will grow another head, but he will keep his pattern of shooting lasers from the north and south.

Use the Cane of Byrna or the Magic Cape if Link has collected either. If not, continue with just the Master Sword. Ignore attacking the floating heads, as they cannot be defeated, and attack the head on the body.

Link will need to detach three heads from the body in order to defeat Blind.

Once Blind has been defeated, collect the Piece of Heart and the Crystal containing the fourth maiden. She will tell Link of the Knights of Hyrule, his ancestors.

Ice Palace

Total Life   15

Heart Pieces   19.75/24

The fifth maiden is locked away in Ice Palace. Located in the Dark World's version of Lake Hylia, Ice Palace is filled with puzzles to open doors and enter rooms. Often, Link will need to return to previous rooms in order to unlock future rooms. This dungeon is all about fire power, so watch the Magic Meter and use the Fire Rod.

Now that Link has acquired the Titan's Mitt, both the Ice Palace and Misery Mire can be completed. Although the Ice Palace is listed as the fifth dungeon in the Dark World, it does not have to be completed before the sixth dungeon, Misery Mire. Getting the dungeon item, the Cane of Somaria, from Misery Mire will allow Link to use a slight shortcut in Ice Palace.

The Tempered Sword (Optional)

Walk south, through the southern gate of the Village of Outcasts and turn left. Lift up a skull and slash the flowers to speak with the frog. This frog has been transformed from a person due to the Dark World's curse. He begs Link to take him back to his partner in Kakariko Village. The frog will begin to follow Link.

Return to the Village of Outcasts by using the southern gate. Exit the village from the pathway to the right.

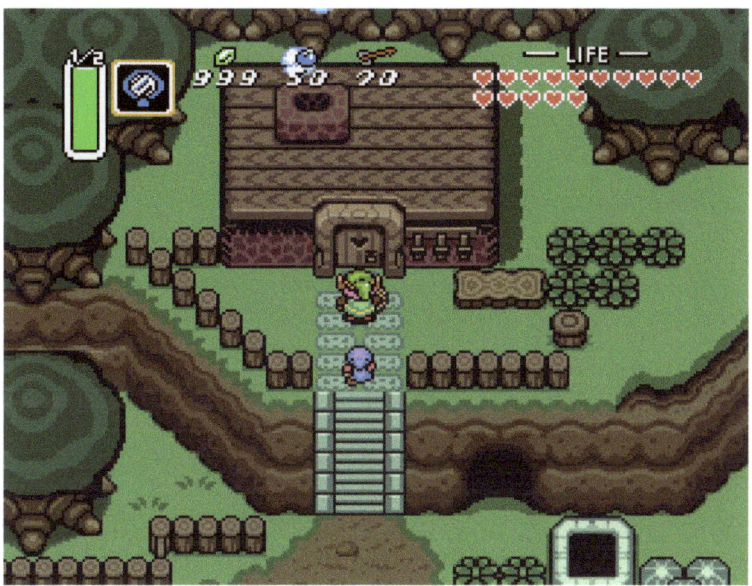

Use the Magic Mirror to teleport back to the Light World. The frog will transform back into a swordsmith. Enter the house to the north.

Walk into the room to reunite the two partners.

Exit the house and re enter. Speak to one of the swordsmiths and he will offer to temper Link's sword in exchange for ten rupees. Pay the rupees and exit the house.

Travel left into Kakariko Village, then back to the right to return to the house. Speak to a swordsmith to get the Tempered Sword. This is an upgrade to the Master Sword that allows it to deal more damage.

Extra Items 3 (Optional)

Use the portal created by the Magic Mirror to return to the Dark World. Lift the large, dark boulders. To the right are twenty two stakes. Use the Magic Hammer to whack them down.

A stump to the south will collapse in on itself, revealing a hole in the earth. Enter and collect the Piece of Heart.

Exit the cave and walk into the house where the swordsmith would be if Link were in the LIght World. Inside, try to open the treasure chest. Link will be unable to open it and the treasure chest will begin to follow him. Do not use a dash attack as this will cause the treasure chest to remain stationary.

Stand to the left of the two large dark boulders and use the Magic Mirror to teleport to the Light World. Use the Flute to warp to Location #7, the Swamp Ruins. Travel left, towards the desert in front of Desert Palace.

Before the grass turns to sand, a man sits to the north of the path. Speak with hima and agree not to tell his secret.

In return, the man will open the treasure chest and Link will receive his fourth Magic Bottle. This is the final Magic Bottle that Link can collect.

Use the Flute to warp to Location #6, the Desert. Lift the dark boulder to the right. Step into the portal to the Dark World.

Jump off of the ledge to the north and continue northward.

Enter the odd looking structure. Two treasure chests inside contain rupees and a Piece of Heart. Move the blocks out of the way to reach the treasure chests.

Exit the cave. Travel right and to the north to find a patch of earth in the corner. Use the Magic Mirror to teleport to the Light World.

Lift the large boulder to reveal a cave.

Inside the cave, push the blocks out of the way to reach the treasure chest and receive the Piece of Heart.

Entering Ice Palace

From the Light World, use the Flute to teleport to Location #8, Lake Hylia. Jump into the lake and swim left to the island containing the cave with the Pond of Happiness. Lift the dark boulder on the center of the island and use the portal to travel to the Dark World.

Enter Ice Palace.

Ice Palace Dungeon Compass

The first portion of the palace will require some Magic. Make sure that Link's Magic Meter is at half or more. In the first room, a Freezor will pop out of the left side of the north wall. Use the Fire Rod to defeat the Freezor and travel through the newly opened door.

The southern Blue Bari holds the key to open the next door. Defeat it, collect the key, and travel through the door to the north.

At the southern end of the hallway is a tile switch. Step on it and enter the newly opened door.

Push the center block to the right and enter the door to the south.

The next room is filled with Pengators. It is optional to defeat the Pengators, but this can be easily accomplish by using the Bombos or Quake Medallion. If Link does defeat them, a treasure chest will appear containing the Dungeon Compass. Travel back through the door to the north.

Ice Palace Dungeon Map

The five blocks will have reset. Push the center block to the north. Step on the tile switch to the right and enter the right door.

In this room, the southern skull hides a switch. It may be easiest to defeat the enemies with the Bombos Medallion before finding and stepping on the switch. Travel back to the room with the five blocks by exiting back through the door to the left.

Step on the floor switch again and push the center block to the left. Next, head through the door to the north.

Defeat the two Red Bari to the south, slash the crystal switch to lower the blue blocks, and defeat the two Red Bari to the north. Place a Bomb next to the crystal switch and walk to the north end of the room. The blue blocks will rise and the red blocks will lower. Toss a Bomb into the center of the room and jump into the hole in the floor.

Lift a skull and defeat the two Stalfos Knights that fall from the north and south ceilings. Enter the door that opens to the south.

The floor moves in the next room and Blade Traps create walls. Babasus float around the room and there are four Blue Baris. The second Blue Bari from the right carries a small key

Collect the small key, make sure the crystal switch is red, and exit through the left door on the southern wall.

A skull to the south against the left wall hides a switch. Step on it and exit through the newly opened door to the right.

Travel through the door to the north.

All of the Pengators in this room must be opened for the northern door to open. This is easily done with the Bombos or Quake Medallion. Exit through the newly opened door.

Wait in the doorway for the Giant Blade trap to return to the north end of the room. Move quickly through the open door to the left.

Avoid the Guruguru Bar and walk down the stairs.

Fall down the hole on the right side of the room.

Walk through the open door to the right.

A Freezor will lump out of the northern wall on the left side. Avoid or defeat it and head through the door to the right.

The closest skull to the north hits a small key. Lift up the pot and collect it. Four skulls circle the center of the room. Lift the block to the north and right to reveal a switch. Step on it and exit through the southern door

The floor is slippery ice here. Be cautious and avoid the Guruguru bar to reach the opened door to the left. If this is a struggle, the Magic Cape can be used, however, be careful about how much Magic it uses.

The skull to the south hides a floor switch. Step on it and a treasure chest containing a small key will appear. Collect the key and enter the door to the north.

Avoid or defeat the enemies and enter the other door on the north wall.

Move quickly to avoid the traps and enemies in this room. The Magic Cape can be used here as well. Travel through the door to the north and right.

Use the Hookshot to defeat the four Red Baris as necessary. Pull Link across the gap by grabbing the far block with the Hookshot. Exit through the door to the south.

Quickly run past the Giant Blade traps to enter the door to the left along the northern wall.

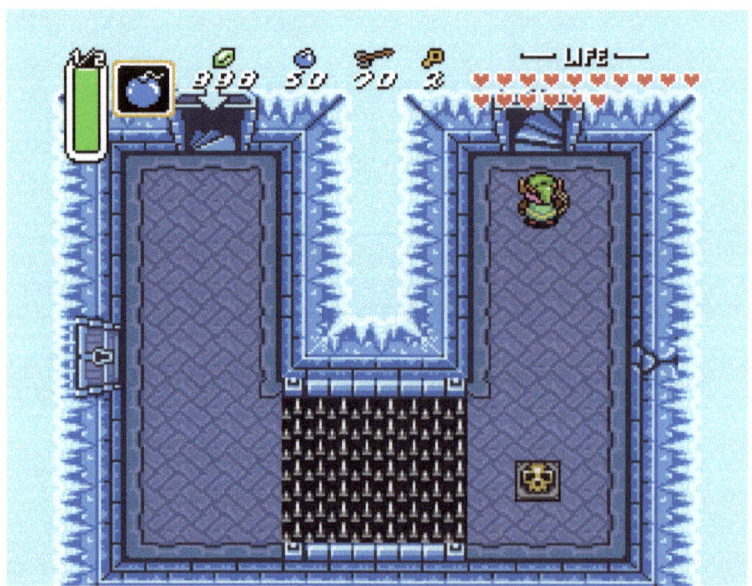

Avoid or defeat the Blue Baris. Use the Hookshot with the skull to pull Link across the spikes in the floor. Exit through the door to the north.

Defeat the Stalfos Knight and use the Magic Hammer to whack the mole heads. Lift the large block and collect the small key. Whack the mole heads on the left. Pull the tongue of the statue to open the door to the right.

Optionally, the most southern skull to the left hides a switch. Stepping on this switch will cause a treasure chest to appear. Open the treasure chest to obtain the Dungeon map. Exit through the newly opened door.

The Blue Mail

Climb up the steps.

Lift the skulls and open the treasure chest to receive the Big Key.

Go back down the steps and pull the tongue of the statue. Return through the door to the left.

Travel through the door to the north.

Lift the skull and step on the switch. A Treasure chest will appear. Use the Hookshot to pull Link to the treasure chest. Open it to receive a small key. Open the door to the left.

Move quickly, past the Giant Blade Trap to the door to the left.

Walk back down the stairs.

Defeat the two Freezors and a treasure chest containing Bombs will appear. Place a bomb in the center of the left wall to make a hole in the floor appear. Fall into the hole.

Open the large treasure chest to receive the Blue Mail. This is an upgrade from Link's standard Green Jerkin. It reduces the amount of damage Link takes by half. When Link wears it, his tunic turns blue and his hat turns yellow.

Push the center block to the right. Next, push the south or north block to the right and exit the room through the open door.

Opening Ice Palace Boss Room

Avoid or Defeat the Freezor and enter the door to the north.

Again, avoid or defeat the enemies and continue north.

Travel south.

IF MISERY MIRE HAS ALREADY BEEN DEFEATED: Lift the skull and place use the Cane of Somaria to place a block on the switch. Skip to the section in the guide titled "Finding Ice Palace Boss Room".

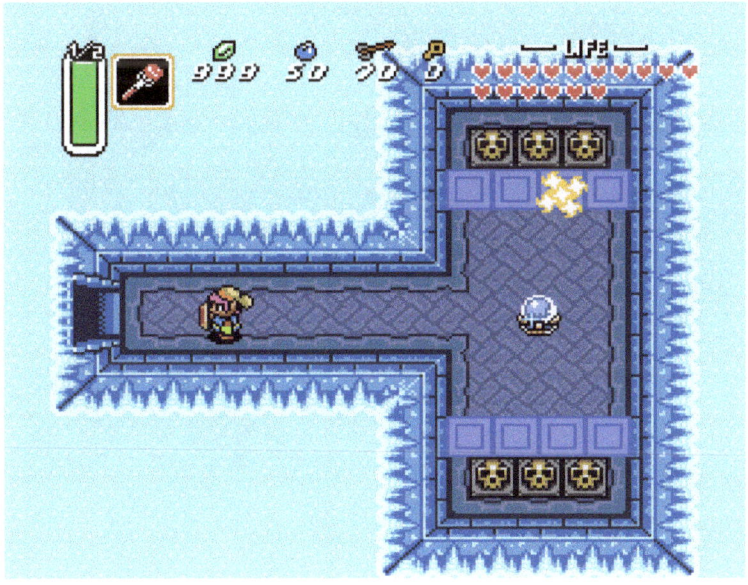

IF MISERY MIRE HAS NOT BEEN DEFEATED: Open the door to the right and enter. Slash the crystal switch to lower the blue blocks.

Travel back one room to the left, then through the door to the north.

With the blue block now lowered, Link can fall through the floor. These lead to a Faerie Spring.

From the room with the two holes in the floor and blue blocks, travel south.

Take the door to the right.

Uncover the switch beneath the upper right skull and enter the door to the south.

Carefully pass the Guruguru again and enter the door to the left.

Travel north.

Quickly run to the door on the right against the northern wall.

The closest skull to the right hides a switch. Step on it, then enter the newly opened door to the left.

Fall into the hole.

Enter the door to the right.

Now that Link is on the left side or the red blocks, push the lower regular block into the hole in the floor. Jump into the hole.

Four Blue Baris are now in the room. Defeat them along with a Freezor and a Stalfos Knight. Lift the skull to reveal a switch. Push the block onto th the switch to open a door to the south.

Finding Ice Palace Boss Room

Travel through the door to the south.

On the left side of the room, lift the pots and pull the statues north. Use the Hammer to whack down the mole heads and lift the large block. Drop in the hole to enter the Boss Room.

BOSS BATTLE Kholdstare

Ice Palace is guarded by Kholdstare, a large white ball that is encased in ice. Kholdstare begins as an unmoving block of ices while balls of ice drop from the ceiling. Ignore the falling pieces and focus on thawing Kholdstare. Link can use the Bombos Medallion once or the Fire Rod eight times.

Once the ice around Kholdstare has melted, Kholdstare will split into three balls. To defeat them,. Use either the Fire Rod or the Tempered Sword. While the sword is easier to use, the Fire Rod requires fewer hits. The tempered sword will take six hits, while the Fire Rod only needs four. Ice balls will continue to fall from the ceiling. Again ignore and avoid them. The Cane of Byrna can be used to protect Link from the falling ice balls while slashing with the Tempered Sword.

After Kholdstare has been defeated, collect the Piece of Heart and the Crystal. The fifth maiden will thank Link and tell him about the powers held by the descendants of the seven wise men.

Misery Mire

Total Life   17

Heart Pieces   22.5/24

After using the Ether Medallion to enter Misery Mire, Link must rescue the sixth maiden from the dungeon boss, Vitreous. I find Vitreous, Link will need to collect the Cane of Somaria. It is hidden behind the puzzles and enemies of Misery Mire.

If Link has not already collected the Ether Medallion, he must do so before entering Misery Mire. There are no extra items to obtain before entering the sixth Dark World dungeon.

Entering Misery Mire

Use the Magic Mirror at the entrance of the Ice Palace to return to the Light World. Next, use the Flute to travel to Location #6, the Desert. Lift the dark boulder to the right and step onto the Dark World portal.

Travel north and slightly right to a platform marked with the symbol or the Ether Medallion.

Stand on top of the symbol and use the Ether Medallion to open the entrance to Misery Mire.

Misery Mire Dungeon Compass

Follow the narrow hallway north and to the right, defeating the Zols that appear. Use the Hookshot to cross the hole in the floor and travel through the doorway.

All of the Popos and Wizzrobes in this room must be defeated for the northern door to open. Avoid the Beamos and enter the door to the north as soon as it opens.

The main room of Misery Mire is a slight maze. The first door Link must enter is the second door from the right on the northern wall. Go down the stairs and travel in the general direction of the door, lifting skulls out of the way as necessary.

In this next room, push the block right or left and the northern door will open. Enter it.

Walk north to reach a treasure chest containing a small key.

Return to the main room of Misery Mire. Walk to the left through the maze and climb the stairs to the top floor. Enter the locked door to the south on the left wall.

The Blue Bari in this room holds a small key. Collect it, slash the crystal switch to turn it blue, and travel through the door to the left.

Twenty two Flying Tiles rise from the floor. Avoid them.

It is optional to light all four torches using the Lamp. Doing so will open the norther door leading to a treasure chest containing the Dungeon Compass.

Cane of Somaria

In the room with the Flying Tiles, travel through the southern door.

Quickly enter the door just to the right on the northern wall.

Stay close to the wall to avoid the holes in the floor. This room is a mirror image to the room through the southern door. In both rooms, the blocks must be moved so that Link has access to the torches. Push the northern and southern blocks towards the torch. Next, move the middle block north or south. Repeat this for all of the blocks in both rooms.

Once paths to the torches have been cleared, quickly light all four torches in both rooms. This will cause a large wall in the next room to move, giving Link access to a hole in the floor. Exit the southern room through the door to the right.

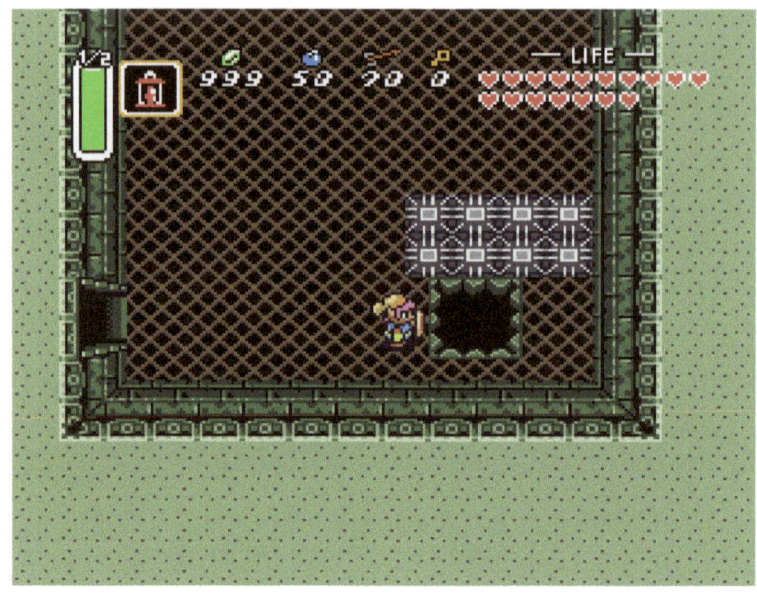

Drop down into the hole in the floor.

Open the treasure chest to receive the Big Key, then exit through the door to the left.

Use the portal on the floor to teleport to a room containing Wizzrobes.

Avoid or defeat the enemies and travel through the right door.

Quickly enter the door to the south, carefully avoiding the enemies.

Avoid the Red Stalfos and Medusas and enter the open door to the right.

Back in the main room of Misery Mire, use the stairs to the right. Cross the maze to return towards the dungeon entrance. Do not exit the dungeon, but enter the door to the right of the dungeon entrance.

Continue right.

The floor in this room will quickly begin to disintegrate. Use the Hookshot on the block, then travel across the narrow path northwards.

Open the large treasure chest to obtain the Cane of Somaria. This item allows Link to conjure blocks. If Link uses the cane on a block that he has created, that block will burst into flames, breaking and shooting in four perpendicular directions.

Misery Mire Dungeon Map

Travel through the door to the right. The treasure chest in here contains the Dungeon Map. Optionally collect it, then head through the door to the north.

If the blue block are raised, jump down to the south, climb the steps, and go through the door to the left. Back in the main room of Misery Mire, climb down to the maze, then enter the door to the north that leads to the room with the single block. Go through the door to the right.

Finding Misery Mire Boss Room

In this room, a small key is hidden beneath the pot on the left of the north wall. There is another small key in this room that is unnecessary, but will give Link access to a room filled with rupees. To collect it, use the Magic Cape and lift the skull in the spikes. Step on the switch and the treasure chest containing the small key will appear. After collecting at least one small key in this room, travel through the northern door.

Walk down the stairs and through the door to the left.

Climb up the steps in the center of the room and unlock the door with the Big Key.

Follow the path north, through an open door.

Here, the room is darkened. Near the left wall is a skull hiding a switch. Lift it, then use the Cane of Somaria to place a block on top of it. This will open a door just to the south.

If Link collected an extra key, there is another door along the southern wall to the right. Open it to gain entrance into a room filled with blue rupees.

Travel through the door opened by the Cane of Somaria.

In another darkened room, Link must travel through an open door to the left. The large block in the center of the room can be lifted to help Link avoid enemies.

The third darkened room is a maze, with Blade Traps, skulls, and moving floors. On the north side of the room is a crystal switch. Use the Boomerang to turn it red. Next, go through the door to the left.

On the north wall of the fourth darkened room is a crack. Use a bomb to blow it open and enter.

To the left is a crystal switch. Hit it to turn it blue, then return through the hole in the wall.

Travel through the door to the left.

Finally in a room with lights, travel to the far north side of the room to find another crystal switch. Hit it to turn it red, then travel through the opening just south of the crystal switch.

Walk left to find the doorway to the Boss Room.

BOSS BATTLE Vitreous

Vitreous is the large, oozing eyeball that guards Misery Mire. Like many enemies in the Legend of Zelda franchise, its weak point is its eye. Good thing Vitreous is almost all eyeball.

For the first portion of the battle, Vitreous will remain stationary. It is protected by a group of smaller eyes. These smaller eyes will attack Link. The Cane of Byrna can be used to defend against their attacks. These eyeballs can be defeated with the Tempered Sword, Arrows, or the Hookshot. While the arrows require the fewest hits (just three), the Tempered Sword is the easiest to use. The easiest way to defeat the smaller eyes is to stand in the bottom right corner, face north, and slash the sword.

Vitreous can also shoot lightning during the first phase of battle. This lightning will move directly south. When Vitreous is about to shoot lightning, the slime surrounding it drips down and exposes the white of the eye. Link cannot defend against this attack, so it is best to move right or left to avoid it.

Once all but four of the smaller eyes have been defeated, Vitreous will bounce towards Link. While the Tempered Sword takes sixteen hits to defeat Vitreous, Arrows only take eight. It is best to stand directly south of Vitreous and shoot arrows until it has been defeated.

Collect the Piece of Heart and Crystal once Vitreous has been defeated. The sixth maiden will speak of Ganon and how he used the seven maidens to break the seal. She also tells Link that Princess Zelda is inside Turtle Rock.

Turtle Rock

Total Life   18

Heart Pieces   22.5/24

Princess Zelda is the seventh and final maiden trapped by Agahnim and Ganon. She is located in Turtle Rock, guarded by a three headed monster called Trinexx. In order to reach the princess, Link must have the Quake Medallion, the Ice Rod, and the Fire Rod. In the dungeon, he will find the Mirror Shield, the final shield upgrade.

The Super Bomb

Once outside of Misery Mire, use the Magic Mirror to teleport to the Light World. Travel to Link's House by using the Flute to teleport to Location #4. Walk south, into the Great Swamp. Follow the cliff to the left, whack the stakes, lift the boulder, and use the portal to the Dark World.

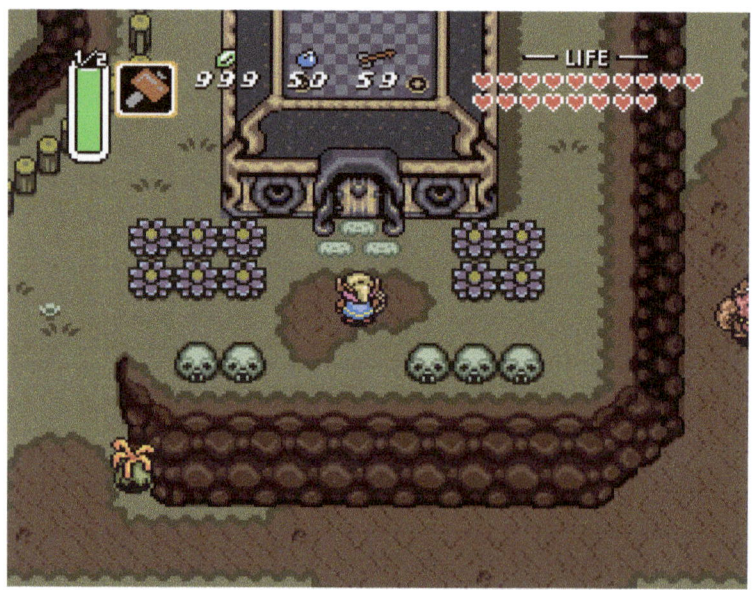

Back in the Dark World, travel north to where Link's House would be in the Light World. Enter the hut.

Inside, the person will sell Link the Super Bomb. Buy it for one hundred rupees and it will begin to follow Link. Do not jump while the Super Bomb is following LInk. This will cause it to explode. If Link uses a dash attack, the Super Bomb will be left behind.

Link must take the Super Bomb to the Pyramid of Power. The easiest and fastest way is to follow the path to the right from the hut, whack the stakes to the north, and continue north along the left side near the water. Take the narrow path left to reach the pyramid.

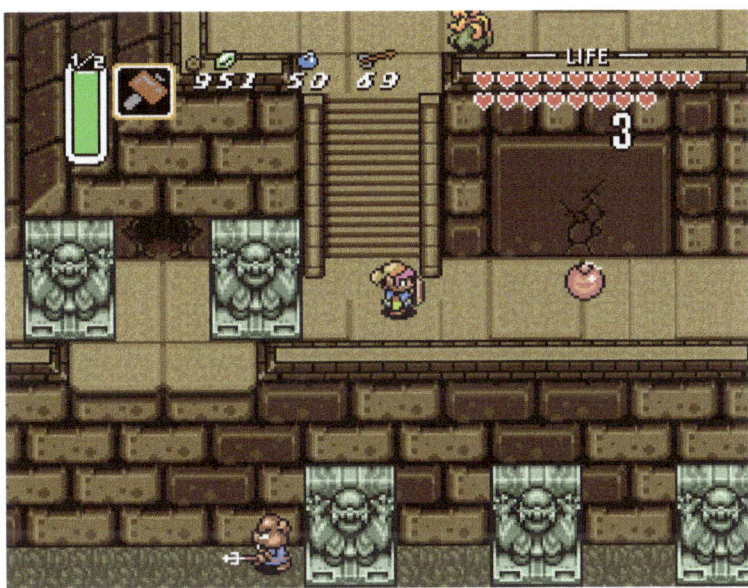

Once at the Pyramid of Power, walk up the central stairs. Go left to a crack in the wall. Leave the Super Bomb here and it will blow open a hole in the wall.

The Golden Sword and Silver Arrows

In this cave is another Mysterious Pond, but it is guarded by an overweight fairy who blames Ganon for her figure.

This time, throw in the Tempered Sword to receive the Golden Sword. This is the final upgrade for the Master Sword and it is eight times more powerful than the Fighter's Sword.

Toss in the Bow and the fairy will give Link the Silver Arrows. This is an upgrade to the regular Arrows and is necessary in the final battle against Ganon

Link can also toss in an empty bottle to receive a bottle filled with Green Potion.

Climbing to Turtle Rock

Use the Magic Mirror to return to the Light World. Travel to Death Mountain, Location # 1 from the Flute. Travel to the right to reach the bridge and use the Hookshot to get across the gap.

Walk south and lift the dark boulder. Step onto the portal to teleport to the Dark World.

To the right, there are two caves on the northern mountain wall. Enter the cave on the left.

Go through the opening at the left end of the hallway.

Keep following the narrow passage and fall into the hole in the floor.

Push the block to the north and exit this area through the door to the left.

Fall through the hole to the right.

Keep traveling right, through an open doorway.

Fall down the southern hole.

Rupees and Bombs are in the treasure chests. It is optional to open them. Move the blocks out of the way and walk through the door on the left.

Exit the cave through the opening to the south.

Extra Items 4 (Optional)

Life the large boulder, revealing a hole in the ground. Enter the hole.

Walk north to the skull. Defeat the Blue Bari to the left. Use the Hookshot to attach to a skull on the left.

Use the Hookshot to attach to the skull on another platform to the south. Open the first treasure chest.

Return to the previous platform by using the Hookshot. Return back to the skull near the entrance. Walk north into the back area. The is a hidden floor here. Use the Hookshot to pull Link towards the skull to the left. Open the second treasure chest.

Pull Link to the treasure chest to the south, towards the left. Open the third treasure chest.

Hookshot over to the skull on the left, walk south, defeat the Blue Bari, and pull Link over to the fourth treasure chest. Open it.

Return to the previous platform. Defeat the Blue Hardhat Beetle and use the Hookshot on the nearby skull. Travel to the platform to the right, then south, then to the right again to return to the skull near the entrance.

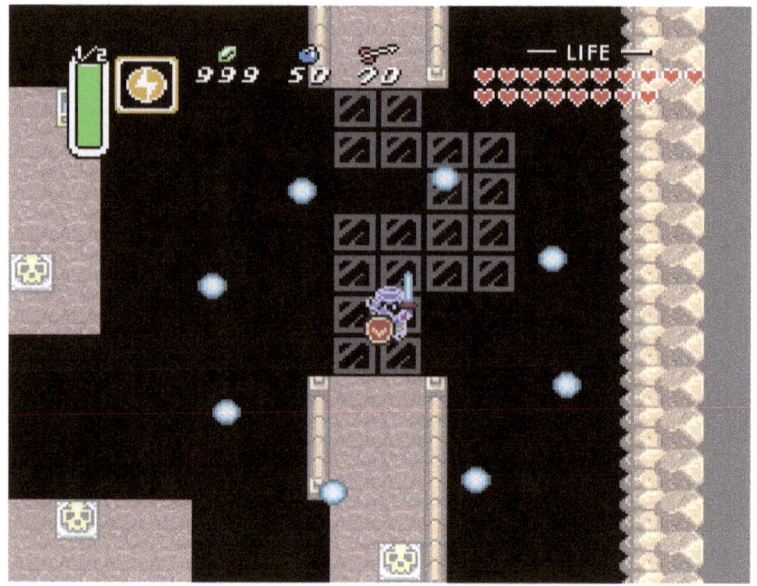

Link can blow open crack to the north of the dark floor by using a Bomb. There is a hidden path to cross. Use the Ether Medallion to reveal the path.

In the next room, the left and north walls and be opened by using a Bomb.

To the north, a fairy will heal Link's Health and Magic.

Travel left to another passageway. Again, the northern wall can be blown open with a Bomb.

Go north to discover a faerie fountain.

Exit the cave through the southern door.

On top of the mountain, use the Magic Mirror to teleport to the Light World. Collect the Piece of Heart and enter the Magic Mirror's warp point to return to the Dark World.

Backtrack all the way through the cave.

Entering Turtle Rock

Use the Magic Mirror to enter the Light World. Travel north and to the right to reach a large dark boulder blocking a stairway. Lift the boulder out of the way and walk up the stairs.

Use the Magic Hammer to whack the stakes down. They need to be whack in the correct order: right, up, and left. A Dark World Portal will appear in the center of the stakes. Enter it.

The Quake Medallion symbol is marked on the ground.

Stand on top of it and Use the Quake Medallion. The head of the turtle will disappear, revealing the entrance to Turtle Rock. Jump off of the ledge to enter.

Inside Turtle Rock, lift the skulls to receive a Green Potion and Bomb. Use the Cane of Somaria on the small block marked with a question mark. This will create a moving platform. Step onto it, then continue north to the next room. This is the main room of Turtle Rock.

Turtle Rock Dungeon Compass (Optional)

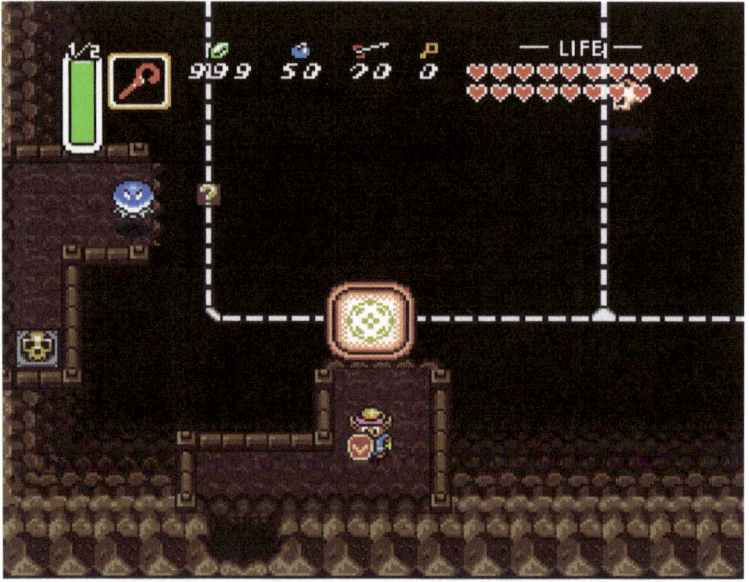

Use the cane on another question mark and travel to the nearest question mark to the left. Go through the door to the south.

Collect the Dungeon Compass from the treasure chest and use the Magic Mirror to return to the beginning of the dungeon. Return to the main room of Turtle Rock.

Turtle Rock Dungeon Map

Use the Cane of Somaria on the question mark. Travel to the second question mark to the right. Enter the open door.

Create a platform with the Rod of Somaria and ride it to the right. There are four torches in this room that must be lit at the same time. To do this, use the Fire Rod when the platform is on the inner track. The two southern torches can be lit at once (from the left side) and the northern torches can be lit individually.

Quickly run through the door to the north before the torches go out.

In this next room, avoid the Spiked Rollers. If this seems too difficult, the Mage Cape can be used. Open the treasure chest on the right for a small key. The Treasure chest on the lift contains the Dungeon Map. Return to the main room of Turtle Rock.

The Mirror Shield

Create another platform and travel to the second door on the north wall. Unlock it with the small key.

Defeat the Hokkubokku and it will drop a small key. Use it to open the door to the north.

Avoid the Chain Chomps. The Magic Cape can be used here. Hit one of the crystal switches with a Boomerang while standing on the southern side of the red blocks. Move one of the northern block in the two groups of five block by the southern door. This will cause a chest to appear. Hit the Crystal switch again, turning it back to red. Open the treasure chest, collect the small key, and exit through the door to the north.

Travel south and to the right in this room. Climb the stairs and enter the pipe to the left. Link will be transported to a door just left of where he originally entered the room. Go through the door.

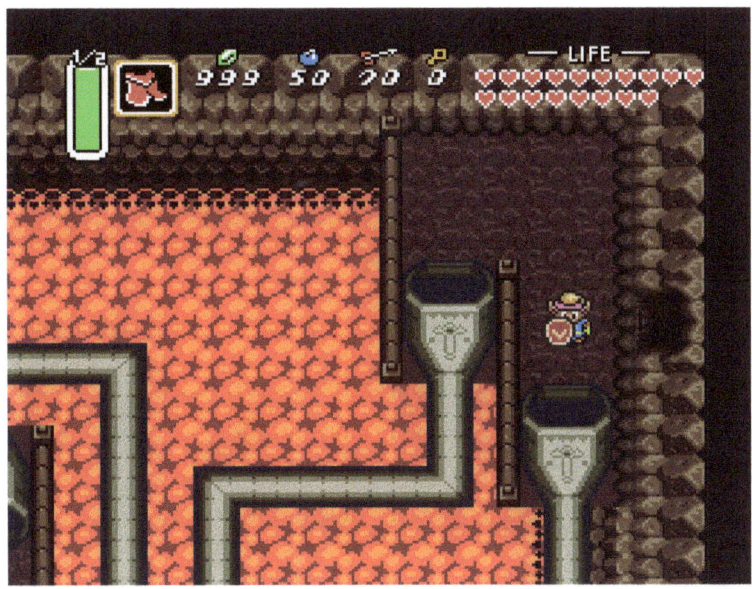

Take the pipe on the right to reach the left side of the room. Walk through the door to the left.

There are many enemies, but the Hokkubokku drops a small key. Hit the crystal switch to turn it blue, defeat the Hokkubokku, collect the small key, and exit through the locked door to the right. Be quick to avoid the Laser Eye above the door.

Use the pipe to travel to the center of the room. Unlock the treasure chest to receive the Big Key. Take the pipe to the south and exit through the door to the right.

Travel through the pipe, then jump off of the ledge. Go up the stairs immediately to the south and enter another pipe. It will transport Link to the northern left corner of this room again.

This time, take the pipe to the left. Next, go through the door to the south.

Both Hokkubokus must be defeated for the door to open. After they had been defeated, travel through the door to the south.

Walk through the left door.

Five Laser Eyes shoot lasers from the northern wall. Avoid them and us a Bomb on the crack in the southern wall. Go through the entrance.

Now outside of Turtle Rock, there is an optional Piece of Heart. Walk to the doorway to the right, Before entering, use the Magic Mirror to teleport to the Light World. Enter the cave. Inside, defeat all four Gori-yaswith the sword and Bow, go through the newly opened door, and unlock the chest to receive the Piece of Heart. Exit the cave and use the Magic Mirror's pwarp point to return to the Dark World.

Enter the door to the right to head back inside of Turtle Rock.

Use either the Cane of Somaria or the Hookshot to reach the large treasure chest. Open it and collect the Mirror Shield. This item is the final shield upgrade and it can reflect the lasers sent from the Laser Eyes. Exit through the door to the north.

Finding Turtle Rock Boss Room

Continue north.

Enter the pipe and travel through the door on the northern wall.

Defeat another Hokkubokku and use Bombs to blow open the crack on the right and northern walls.

Optionally, the hole to the right leads to a room filled with rupees. Lift both skulls, then push the northern block to the left. Pull the tongue of the statue to the left and enter the newly opened door. Avoid the Spiked Rollers, collect the ruppes, and exit back two rooms.

Continue through the door to the north.

Step into the path of the Spiked Roller, quickly hit the crystal switch with the Boomerang, and open the treasure chest to collect a small key. Once again, step into the path of the Spiked Roller and hit the crystal switch. Exit through the locked door to the north.

Create a platform and head right. Immediately turn south and hold the controller to the south so that Link continues in the same direction at each fork.

Lift the skull and step on the switch. Return to the created platform travel north. Once the platform begins to move, hold the controller to the left. Exit through the door to the south.

Use the Magic Cape or carefully use the dash attack to defeat the enemies as Link runs southward. Be careful to to fall off the ledge at the end if the dash attack is used. Exit through the southern door.

Again, use the Magic Cape or dash attack to reach the south end of the room. Ignore the treasure chests. They only contain rupees and are not worth the trouble due to the Laser Eyes in the room. Use a Bomb on the southern wall and enter the new opening. Link will be outside the dungeon, on a small platform. Re enter the dungeon through the same door. The purpose of this is that Link will respawn at this entrance if he loses full life or uses the Magic Mirror. If this exit is not used, Link would be teleported to the very beginning of Turtle Rock.

Carefully defeat the Hardhat Beetle. Walk towards the treasure chest to the left, using the Mirror Shield to deflect the Laser Eye's attack. Collect the small key, then exit through the door at the north end of the room.

Enter the locked door to the left.

Use the Magic Powder on the Anti-Fairy and defeat the Helmasaur. Walk to the second square area along the south wall. Use the boomerang to hit the crystal switch to the right and turn it blue.

Move one more square area to the left and use the Boomerang on the crystal switch to the north to turn it red.

Walk north two squares, left one, north again, and left again. Use the boomerang on the switch to the left blue and exit the room through the door to the north.

Create a platform and travel north to reach the Boss Room.

BOSS BATTLE Trinexx

Trinexx has three heads: a main head, a blue head that spits ice, and a red head that spits fire. The ice from the blue head will stick to the ground causing it to become slippery. For this reason, the blue head should be defeated first. The blue and red heads must be stunned and then attack. To stun them, use the Fire rod on the blue head and the Ice Rod on the red head. Once the head has been stunned, attack it with the sword.

Occasionally, the main head will stretch out and attack Link. Trinexx begins to swing its tail rapidly before this move, so try to move out of the way.

Once the blue and red head have been defeated, Trinexx will break out of its shell and move around the room. Use the Golden Sword to slash at the flashing section in the center of its body. It will take three hits to defeat Trinexx.

After Trinexx has been defeated, collect the Piece of Heart and the final Crystal that contains Princess Zelda. She warns Link that Ganon is waiting in his tower to pass through the gate between the worlds. Once Ganon passes into the Light World, he will be undefeatable, she says. Princess Zelda encourages Link to beat him before he leaves the Dark World.

Ganon's Tower

Total Life   20

Heart Pieces   24/24

With all seven maidens rescued, Link has enough combined power to open Ganon's Tower. Before Ganon can be defeated, Link must collect the Red Mail, battle all three Light World bosses, and face Agahnim a second time.

There is nothing left for Link to collect in the overworld, so he can go directly to Ganon's Tower. Once inside the tower, there are two directions Link can explore. Both sides will take Link to the same end point. The right side of the tower is more difficult and leads to the Dungeon Compass. The left side of the tower is recommended and leads to the Dungeon Map. Since there is no reason to obtain the Dungeon Compass, that entire right section of the tower can be ignored.

Finding Ganon's Tower

Ganon's Tower is located where the Tower of Hera would be in the Light World. To reach the tower, travel left from Turtle Rock. Go south, to the hole in the ground, and continue left. Cross the narrow bridge.

Continue left to reach Ganon's Tower. Walk to the center of the tower and the seven maidens will break the seal, opening a stairwell. Enter the dungeon.

Entering Ganon's Tower

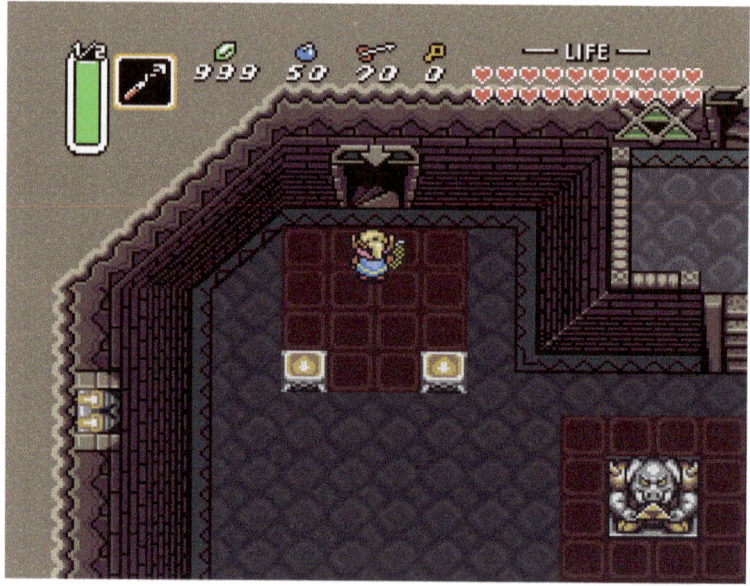

Take the door on the left.

Use a dash attack to collect the key from on top of the right torch. Travel through the door to the left.

The skull nearest to Link hides a small key under it. Collect the small key. The mole heads in the room surround a block. This block needs to move in any direction. Whack at least two blocks to move the block. This will cause the holes in the floor to disappear and the door to the left to open. Travel through the newly opened door.

Link will need to use the Hookshot to reach the southern platform. Pull Link to the block to the left, lift the skull out of the way, then travel to the next platform to the south.

Next, use the block to the left and travel to the south, being careful to avoid the Blade Trap. Avoid or defeat the Red Stalfos and use the skulls to pull Link to the south.

Ganon's Tower Dungeon Map (Optional)

Travel through the locked door to the right to collect the Dungeon Map. Avoid the two Guruguru Bars and collect the Dungeon Map from the treasure chest. Exit back through the door to the left.

Finding the Six Armos Knights

Hit the crystal switch to lower the blue blocks. Place a Bomb near a crystal switch and walk to the south of the blue blocks. Once the blue blocks rise, go through the door to the south.

The southern skull has a small key. Midway between the trap and the crystal switch, place either a Bomb or a block (using the Cane of Somaria). Quickly collect the key from the skull before the Bomb explodes. If the Cane of Somaria was used, use the cane again to make the block catch fire. The blue blocks in the room should lower, allowing Link to exit through the door to the left.

Strike the crystal switch, then enter the portal on the right side of the room. Avoid the Blade Traps.

Walk left through the room, avoiding the traps. There is a lone block near the middle. Push it to the two blocks on the left and a treasure chest will appear at the left end of the room. Use the Hookshot on the treasure chest to pull Link across. Open the chest to receive a small key, then exit through the door to the south.

The next few rooms are a maze of warp tiles. Be sure to step on them in the correct order:

1. Right.
2. Left.
3. South
4. Avoid the holes and enemies. Take the tile to the north.
5. North.

Exit through the door to the left.

This is the room where the right (Dungeon Compass) and left (Dungeon Map) paths converge. If The path to the right was traveled, Link would enter this room from the right side. Travel north and to the right to reach two skull pots. Lift the northern skull out of the way, but do not touch the southern one.

Next, travel south, to the left, and north. Use the Fire Rod to light the torch from the pathway to the left. This will show a secret floor in the room. Hookshot over to the skull, then quickly follow the path to reach the door on the right side of the northern wall.

If Link is not quick enough, the torch will extinguish and the floor will become invisible again. Enter through the doorway.

Lift the skull and avoid the Anti-Fairy to open the treasure chest. Collect the Arrows, then place a Bomb over the crack floor near the treasure chest. Fall through the newly opened hole.

MINI BOSS BATTLE Six Armos Knights

Link must face the six Armos Knights from Eastern Palace. This time, however, the floor is ice. A single hit with a Silver Arrow will defeat aArmos Knight. Otherwise, this battle is exactly the same as before.

Once they have been defeated, travel through the door to the north.

Open the treasure chest to collect Arrows, Bombs, and the Big Key. Exit through the door to the south.

The Red Mail

From the room with the six Armos Knights, travel through the door to the left. The northern wall can be opened by using a dash attack or a Bomb. Inside is a Faerie Spring. Be careful not to fall through the hole in the floor when collecting fairies.

Continue through the door to the left on the northern wall.

Push the block to the right, avoid the traps, and open the large treasure chest. Inside is the Red Mail. This is the last upgrade for the Link's tunic and is the last collectable item in the game. The Red mail reduces the damage that Link takes from attack by half compared to the Blue Mail.

Finding the Three Lanmolas

Exit the room through the door to the north.

Continue north.

Back in the first room of Ganon's Tower, climb the stairs to the north and walk through the center door.

The main goal of this room is to move the northern block further to the north. Avoid or defeat the enemies while hitting the crystal switches to create a path left. The Magic Cape can be used in this room to make it easier. Exit through the newly opened door to the south.

Use Arrows to defeat the two Red Goriyas. The statue can be used to block the Blade Traps if necessary. Once both enemies have been defeated, travel through the door to the right.

Avoid the two Beamos and defeat another two Red Goriyas. Exit through the door to the north.

Continue north.

Walk down the stairs and travel north. Hit the crystal switch to make the red blocks lower. This will give the Blade Traps more room to move and will make avoiding them easier. The Magic cape can also be used in this room. At the north end, there are two hidden Eyegores. Avoid them or defeat them. Lift the middle skull and step on a switch.

Return to the stairs at the south, follow the right floorway northward, and exit through the door to the right.

In this room, follow the narrow pathway to the right. Be careful to avoid the Balls shooting out of the walls. The Magic Cape or a well timed dash attack can be used. At the end of the path are two blocks. Face north in front of the blocks and use a dash attack. This will knock Link backwards and onto the platform to the south. Use a Bomb to blow a hole in the wall and enter.

Collect the fairies and break the skulls for Bombs and a Green Potion. Exit the room.

Use the Hookshot to reach the northern platform. Continue through the door to the north.

In the next few rooms, all of the enemies must be defeated. The easiest way to do this is with the Bombos Medallion. Defeat the first room and travel left.

Defeat the three Red Stalfos and go through the door to the south.

The three Blue Zazaks must be defeated, then take the door to the south.

Again, defeat the two Red Zazaks and travel south.

Finally, defeat the Red Zazak and Red Stalfos. Go through the door to the left.

Avoid the Rabbit Beam and continue left.

MINI BOSS BATTLE Three Lanmolas

The only difference in facing the three Lanmolas this time is that there is a Medusa in the room as well. Each Lanmolas will require two slashes with the Golden Sword or one hit with the Silver Arrow.

After the enemies have been defeated, head through the northern door.

Finding Moldorm

Continue north.

Use the Ether Medallion to defeat the three Wizzrobes and illuminate a secret path. The path will disappear as soon as the Ether Medallion is not in use, so memorize it while it's lit up. Exit to the south.

Use the dash attack to cross the narrow path and head through the door to the north.

Defeat the Wizzrobes with the Ether Medallion and exit through the newly opened door to the north.

Again, use the dash attack to follow the narrow path. This should knock the enemies out of the way. The floor here will also disintegrate, so move quickly. Enter the open door to the right.

The first task in this room is to carefully remove all of the skulls. Next, use the Fire Rod to light all four torches.

Once they have been lit, follow the path along the left and southern part of the room to the opened door.

Lift the pot to the right for a Green Potion, then travel up the stairs in the center of the room.

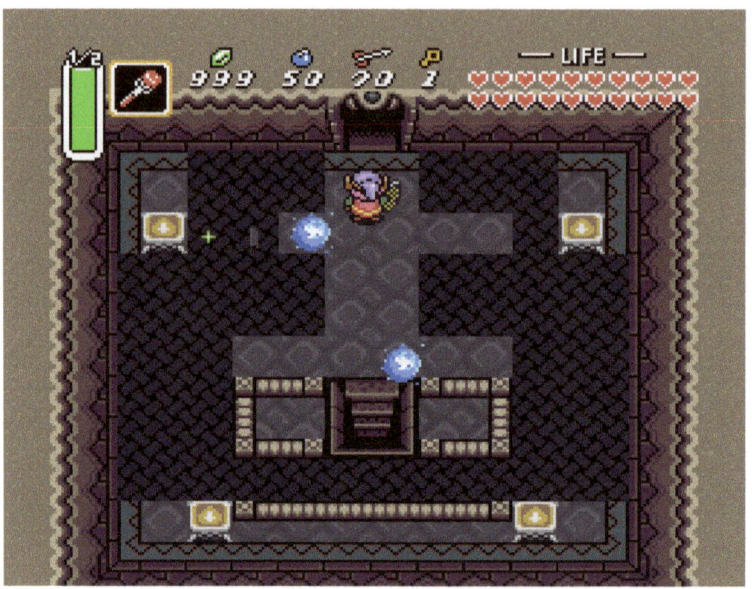

The four torches in this room must be lit all at once with the Fire Rod in order for the door to open. This must be done quickly because the floor disintegrates. The best order to light the torches is bottom right, bottom left, upper left, then upper right. Quickly exit through the northern door.

Defeat the Hardhat Beetles for a small key. Open the treasure chests to collect Bombs, then exit to the left.

A crack on the southern wall must be opened. The easiest way to do this is to throw the Bomb just right of the crack and let the moving floor carry it to the crack. Enter the opening.

Use the Magic Powder to collect the Anti-Fairy first. Then, step next to a crystal switch, between the red and blue blocks. Hit the crystal switch so that the red blocks rise and the blue blocks lower. Open the treasure chest to receive a small key. Walk back between the two types of blocks and hit the crystal switch again. Exit through the southern door.

MINI BOSS BATTLE Moldorm

Jump down from the ledge to start the battle with Moldorm. Moldorm will only require two hits from the Golden Sword to be defeated.

Like the first encounter, Link can be knocked off of the ledge. If this happens, return by going up a set of stairs and restarting the battle.

After Moldorm has been defeated, use the hookshot on the treasure chest to the south. Open it for a red rupee before climbing the stairs. Push the blocks out of the way and exit through the open door.

Finding Agahnim

This room is filled with traps and Hardhat Beetles. The best way to reach the northern end is to use the Magic Cap. Enter the open doorway.

Follow the blue carpet to Agahnim's Boss Room.

BOSS BATTLE Agahnim

While Agahnim's attacks remain the same as when Link first fought him, one thing is drastically different. This time, Agahnim will split into three. The darkest of the Agahnims is the real one, while the translucent ones are distractions. Focus on repelling the attack back to the solid Agahnim while avoiding the shadow Agahnims. The shadow Agahnim's attack can also be repelled back onto the real one. It will take five hits to defeat the real Agahnim.

Once Agahnim has been defeated, Ganon will leave his disguise as Agahnim, turn into a bat, and fly away. Lucky for Link, the Flute duck is nearby to help. As Ganon crashes into the top of the Pyramid of Power, Link is not far behind.

BOSS BATTLE Ganon

Before facing Ganon, make sure Link is fully healed and that his bottles are fully stocked. The Golden Sword and Silver Arrows will make the battle much easier as well. Once everything is ready, drop down into the hole in the Pyramid of Power to face Ganon.

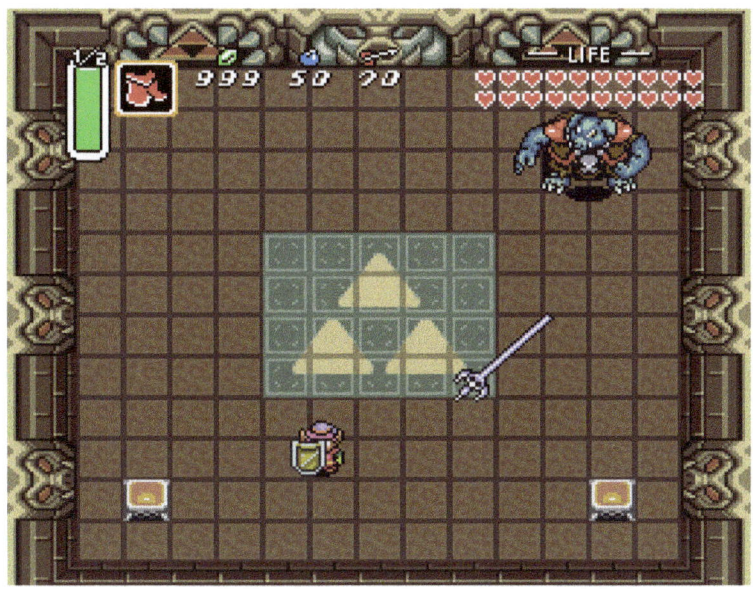

Quickly get in a free sword slash on Ganon before he starts talking. Once the monologue is over, he will spin and throw his Trident while teleporting around the room. Avoid the Trident and hit him with the sword. If Link does not have the Golden Sword, he can only damage Ganon with a spin attack.

Ganon will eventually quit throwing the Trident and begin to emit a spinning ring of fireballs. Each ball will transform into a Blazing Bat and attack Link. Avoid the Blazing Bats and Ganon as much as possible while continuing to slash at him with the sword.

Next, Ganon will summon a single Blazing Bat that leaves a circle of fire behind. Avoid the Blazing Bat and the fire while continuing to slash Ganon.

Hitting him before he is able to summon a Blazing Bat will trigger his next attack. For this, Ganon jumps up and heavily lands on the ground, causing the north portion of the room to collapse. Do not fall into this hole or Link will have to restart the fight. This jumping will happen three more times, with each side of the room collapsing in a clockwise pattern.

When the final portion against the left wall falls, Ganon will extinguish the torches, plunging the room into darkness. He refers to this as his "Technique of Darkness". For the remaining part of the battle, Link must continually light the torches in order to see Ganon.

After Ganon has jumped on the ground for the fourth time, Link can quickly light the bottom left torch before the bottom right torch goes out. If this is done quickly, the bottom right torch will remain lit for the rest of the battle. Link will only need to keep relighting one torch instead of two.

While both torches are lit, Link will need to stun Ganon with a sword slash. Once Ganon turns blue, shoot him with a Silver Arrow. Repeat this four times to defeat him.

Once Ganon has been defeated, go through the door to the north to speak with the Essence of the Triforce.

The Triforce will explain how its power works. As the game ends, the camera will pass by several side characters, showing their happiness now that the Dark World has been destroyed and the Light World is at peace. The Master Sword sleeps again. Until it is called upon by the hero to save the world once more.

I hope you have been enjoying my books.

From one gamer to another please take a minute and write an honest review on the Amazon page for me.

Positive reviews help others purchase and enjoy theses books as well and I LOVE reading them too ☺

If you have any further questions or comments please reach me at blacknesguy@gmail.com

Twitter @blacknesguy
Facebook: facebook.com/theBlackNESguy

To leave a review go here:

http://bit.ly/blacknesguy

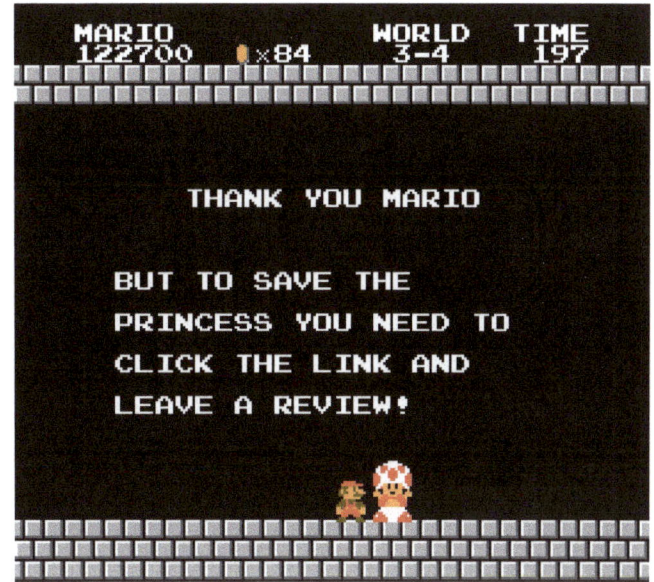

Player 2 Press Start

It's dangerous to go alone. Take this… book for free.

Would you like to get the next book from BlackNES Guy for FREE?

Join my **Player 2 Press Start** team and I'll send you a copy of my next book (ebook) free of charge. The only thing that I ask in return is that if you like it that you please leave a review for it ☺

Game On!

http://bit.ly/Player2startnow

www.ingramcontent.com/pod-product-compliance
Lightning Source LLC
Chambersburg PA
CBHW051256110526
44589CB00025B/2844